The Autobiography of Rose Hacker

Best Wishes to
Elaine Povey
from
Rose Hacker

Deptford Forum Publishing Ltd
441 New Cross Road
London SE14 6TA

First published 1996

Designed by Ed Fredenburgh
Printed by Transart Ltd, 12a Percy Road, Mitcham, Surrey CR4 4JU

ISBN 1 898536 260

British Library Cataloguing in Publication Data
A catalogue record for this book is available from the British Library

FOREWORD

This book was conceived some ten years ago at the instigation of Moira Roth, my 'adopted daughter', who made a series of tape-recordings of interviews with me.

An autobiography is a work of egocentricity – my only claim to interest unknown readers is that I will be ninety on March 3rd 1996, and my memory is fairly intact, covering almost a century of bewildering and rapid change. I have played an active part and experienced personally the rise and fall, the hope and disillusion, of Marxists, Freudians, Humanists, Internationalists and The Welfare State.

The changes in family life and in the relationships between men and women have shattered old certainties, but I still believe that we are social animals, not predators, but we can never cease to work to get the balance right.

ACKNOWLEDGEMENTS

This book would never have been written without Moira Roth, who instigated it by taping interviews with me in the mid-eighties.

Over ten years she encouraged and gently prodded me to overcome my sloth. Every time I visited Moira in the USA, I came home full of creativity and enthusiasm and each time, gradually I resumed my undisciplined life of pleasure and relaxation.

As my ninetieth birthday approached, we felt it was imperative that I finish the autobiography. Moira came to stay with me over Christmas in 1995 and together we undertook the laborious task of editing. She bullied, she insisted, she gave up an entire holiday, working assiduously despite my preference for eating and partying. Miracle of miracles, we finished the book on December 29th. Moira's example of scholarship and diligence has been an inspiration.

I am deeply indebted to my supportive and enthusiastic friend who chose, for various reasons, to be anonymous. It was she who took on the horrendous task of in-putting the original manuscripts onto the computer, heroically interpreting my impossible handwriting and endless corrections.

My sons, daughters-in-law and grandsons have supported and encouraged me unfailingly. There are many friends and relatives to whom I owe an enormous debt; they are too numerous to mention individually, but I do hope when they read this book, they will realise what a major role they have played in my life, and accept my gratitude.

To Moira Roth

CONTENTS

Family Background

Home is the place where
when you have to go there
they have to take you in.
I should have called it
something you somehow
haven't to deserve.
Robert Frost – Death of the Hired Man

"I wish I was dead! I wish I was dead!" I was face down on my bed, crying hopelessly. I was twelve years old and for the first time in my life I had been beaten on my bottom by my father, at my mother's instigation. Father's hands were large, bony, beautiful; provoking fear when they threatened, and sometimes hit, my brother. Girls were rarely punished in this way.

It had been wildly exciting when, already a bookworm, I found a fat, brown paper-covered volume in the cupboard beside my parents' bed. What a treasure! What marvellous pictures! The human body and what was inside. One could lift up cut-out layers to reveal pictures of muscles, bones and internal organs. Best of all of the pictures depicted babies in various stages of growth inside the mother's body, cosily curled up in a womb, then coming out through a tube I never knew existed. How could it stretch to allow the baby to emerge?

These revelations made nonsense of Mother's tales about the doctor and his black bag or the gooseberry bush stories that friends retailed. The sense of wonder and excitement and satisfied curiosity echoed the feelings in botany classes when plants were examined and the reproductive process explained. Why! It was the same with human beings.

Full of this new knowledge, I passed it on to my younger brother and sister. We often wondered how we had been born and now we knew. The younger ones could not keep a secret, nor did they understand why this information should be secret. Our parents' anger was amazing. "How a word can diminish a wonder!", but the wonder of life itself was diminished and I wished myself dead.

* * *

I have not wished for death since this formative event at age twelve. Generally my life has been fulfilling and enjoyable. Any frustrations and difficulties have enhanced the satisfactions.

My father was upwardly mobile and I barely remember a time before we were a typical Jewish suburban family. My father was born in 1875 in a little place called Kalisch, in Russian Poland. His start in life could not have been poorer and he would often remind us of this, saying, "Remember, we come from the poorest slums in Russian Poland." In those days Jews were literally 'beyond the pale'. A minority within a minority, they were persecuted by Poles and Russians alike. They were not allowed into the capital cities, nor into certain trades and professions. They scratched a living taking in each other's washing and plying their little trades. My father was one of eight children in a piteously poor family. Years later my grandmother told me that, when she could not afford to buy things for her children, she would tell them they were not Kosher and therefore forbidden. So the family never ate quite ordinary things, like oranges and bananas, because she could not bear to say that they cost too much. I think, though, that they did have some happy times. My aunt used to tell me stories about the rivers freezing over and how they would meet their boyfriends and

My paternal grandparents on their wedding day, which was in 1870 or possibly earlier

have fun skating over the frozen water. Life is rarely utterly miserable all the time, especially for children.

My father was apprenticed to a book-binder and led quite a Dickensian life. He was made to sleep under the workbench and was given only left-over food from his employer's table. He was never invited in to eat with the boss who was, of course, also Jewish. It was rare for Jews and non-Jews to work with each other. They led a very segregated existence, living in a ghetto little better than a slum. I am often struck by the fact that my father led a terribly hard life yet he was able to create beauty. I have a prayer book which he bound himself, an exquisite object. He even made the marbled end papers, as well as doing the gilded tooled leatherwork.

In 1893 my father left Poland, like so many young men, to escape conscription into the army. He came to London and stayed with a cousin in the tailoring trade. Boyhood memories of persecution remained with him and he nursed a fierce ambition to bring all his family over from Poland to join him in England. He did achieve his aims by working incredibly hard, as did so many immigrants at that time, learning a trade and building up his own business in the fashion trade, known to all who worked in it as the 'rag trade'. He started in a small way by making one or two garments, selling them, putting the money straight back into the business to buy more cloth, then making more garments. Thanks to all his hard work, he became moderately successful. But in those days if a Jew wanted to get on in England he had to present a front that was not Jewish, because 'quality customers' would not even see a common, foreign Jew named Abraham Goldbloom from the East End of London. So my father went into partnership with a Mr Thompson, an impressive-looking Englishman who was always beautifully dressed and had whiskers like King Edward VII. The firm was called Thompson and Goldbloom. My father kept very much in the background and Thompson was the partner who saw the customers. Over the years this gradually changed and my father became persona grata with everybody, and very popular too.

He managed very well on his own when Mr Thompson retired. In spite of friendship between our families there was always an undercurrent of anti-

Semitism and anti-Goyism and jealousy. Thompson had a French wife and she had a little Pekinese dog and one daughter called Dollie. We used to visit and be absolutely entranced because Dollie had so many beautiful dolls with lovely French-style clothes. The Pekinese dog had a satin-lined basket and ate roast beef and cream every day. I was amazed at this extravagance. This was the most pampered peke I've ever known and Dollie was our ideal of perfection, a real English beauty. In those days if you had a car it was quite usual to have a chauffeur, and the Thompson's chauffeur, Arthur, was very good-looking. Dollie fell in love with him and, despite all the parents' opposition, a wedding was arranged. There are photographs in my mother's album of Dollie's grand wedding to the chauffeur. Dollie's father set him up in a motorcar business.

My mother was also Jewish, aspiring to the middle classes and wanting to rise in the world. Born in England, she considered herself very superior to my father who, in her own words, was "just a bloody foreigner!" Although he could speak perfect English, my father had a slight accent which he would exaggerate just to annoy her.

It was hard for me to understand my mother's feelings of superiority. She was born in 1882 to a poor family in the East End of London. Her parents had met and married in the German part of Poland. They seem to have been a little less poor than my father's family, although it was a very similar set-up. I don't think there was as much persecution in German Poland as there was in the Russian part. Nevertheless, the couple found it a struggle to earn a living, so before they settled down to raise a family, grandfather went to stay with relatives in Germany in a bid to find work. This failed and he came to London soon after, where he set himself up as a gentleman's tailor in the East End. And in the East End he stayed, where all his customers, like him, were Jews. Although the shop remained in Commercial Street, as he prospered the family moved to Upper Street, Islington.

Some years ago I went to an exhibition of Jewish life in East London at the Royal Festival Hall, where I saw an old advertisement for my grandfather's shop: "Philip Silverstone, strictly Kosher tailoring". It seems that among orthodox Jews there is a rule about mixing wool with other fabrics. Ready-made clothes would be unpicked to see whether the interlining was made of a prohibited fabric: if so, it would have to be changed. It was strange to have this sudden contact with someone who, though intimately connected to me, I never knew. For Philip Silverstone died young, leaving my grandmother to bring up eight children single-handed. The older ones, especially the girls, had to help with the little ones. Some of them went into the family business and one son died young. The family story had it that his death was due to drinking cold water after strenuous sporting activities!

My maternal grandparents, Philip and Yetta Silverstone

My mother did well at school and won prizes. I still have one, *Daisy* by Susan Warner, a most improving book which I loved as a child. Daisy was a priggish and heroic Christian who disapproved of her parents because they kept slaves and drank alcohol. She tried to convert them to support the North in the American Civil War and to be more religious. The book is inscribed, "Presented to Miss Rebecca Silverstone from her Master, Mr Braveman, for German".

With her bereaved mother struggling to make ends meet, my mother's education ended at the age of twelve and she went to work for a milliner, earning two shillings and sixpence per week, less than thirteen pence in today's currency.

My mother was the third of four girls and with their four brothers the family were always closely knit. My father often remarked that my mother loved her brothers and sisters more than she loved him and her own children. They were always together, visiting each other regularly with their children even between the many actual occasions, births, Bar Mitzvahs, engagements, weddings and funerals.

My mother's creed could be summed up as obedience to your mother and unquestionably copying her way of life. The watchword was duty to your family and your religion. Charitable work was also a duty. A woman's role was strictly defined: to be a good wife and mother and to maintain a comfortable and happy home. Nothing else was necessary. Ambition for your children was to ensure a good job for boys and marriage for girls. Both these aims were to provide entry into a higher and wealthier class. Reading Jane Austen's *Pride and Prejudice,* I saw my mother as Mrs Bennett.

My parents must have met at one of the many family celebrations. Dancing at local weddings or Bar Mitzvahs was the main introduction for boy and girl, often leading to courtship and marriage.

I still have the menu of the dinner to celebrate my parents' wedding held at the Limehouse Town Hall on Wednesday August 17th 1904. They ate well in those days and no *simcha* (celebration) was authentic without a good 'tuck in'. Here is the menu and I think its mixture of languages is fun!

Vermicelli Soup
Filet of Veal – Sauce Citron
Filet de Boeuf au Champignons Green Peas
Giblet Pies
Roast Chicken Roast Gosling
French Beans Pomme de Terre Duchess
Green Peas Olives
Lemon Jelly Wine Jelly
Almond Gateau Cokernut (sic) *Gateau*
Dessert
Hothouse Grapes, Pines, Pears, Bananas
Coffee

My parents were among the very earliest Jewish families to get right away from the East End background; they never lived there. In 1904 they started their married life in a flat over a shoe shop in Great Portland Street. My brother and I were born there. My sister was born in the second family home, a house in Lime Grove, Shepherds Bush, close to the BBC where memories were revived when I went there years later to do a broadcast.

My mother and her sisters had their many children with little or no knowledge of birth control. My mother was appalled at the thought of another child and tried, successfully, to terminate her fourth pregnancy by skipping, jumping down the stairs, taking hot baths and drinking gin. She was quite ill and used to voice her resentment at my father's lack of sympathy for her predicament. She once told me how much she enjoyed sex until the fear of repeated pregnancies 'put her off'. Luckily she seemed unable to conceive after the miscarriage, unlike her sisters and brothers who had larger families. Both my father's and my mother's families were so prolific that I had fifty first cousins. How families have dwindled and diminished: there are now no Goldbloom or Silverstone blood relatives in existence.

The main reason for the social climbing, apart from having a more comfortable home and good clothes, was because your appearance reflected your husband's position and income. Men bought furs and jewels, not necessarily to please their wives but to show how important they were. Another reason for climbing was so that your daughters would marry rich Jewish boys who were up and coming professionally. Preferred professions were medicine, law and accountancy. Anyone pursuing a career as an artist or a musician was considered a bit odd. It reminds me of the old Jewish joke about the boy who wanted to be a rabbi: "Was that a good career for a nice Jewish boy? No, so badly paid!"

* * *

My earliest memories are intense and concentrated, with the atmosphere of a dream remembered upon waking, vivid and emotional. I find it difficult to disentangle events that have become family stories from those I have actually experienced.

In the family album there is a photograph of my brother and sister sitting at each end of a big pram. I always felt deprived because, once my sister came on the scene, I was never comfortably seated in the pram, at least, that is my emotional memory of it. I had to walk everywhere when I was only two and a half. In the photograph I am standing on a stool behind the pram wheels and my mother is removing my hand from my mouth to stop me sucking my thumb. This is an exchange which went on almost all my life; mother always pulling my hand away from my mouth and slapping it. I used to suck my thumb at night in bed but I had to hold a piece of satin ribbon in my hand all the time. I think I can remember once wetting the bed. I thought I was dreaming but woke up to find that I really had. That was a terrible thing to do, a great disgrace.

There goes the thumb!

I remember the following event as it had great significance for me. I must have been about two or three at the time. I was standing in front of a kitchen chair, scribbling on a piece of paper. The maid brought a kettle of boiling water, poured it into a bucket behind where I was standing, then went to the kitchen for some cold water to cool it down. In her absence I stepped back and sat in the bucket of boiling water. I can't remember the feeling of pain but I can remember spending a lot of time lying on my face in the pram in the kitchen and the doctor coming to see me every day. Mother told me that I was so badly scalded that the skin came off as she tried to take off my clothes so I must have spent a long time in that position on my face in the kitchen.

When we moved to Lime Grove I went to a nursery school. The only thing I remember about it is a rocking horse; if you brought a farthing you could have a ride on it.

My first experience of the country is associated with disaster. I was not more than three years old when Father was taken seriously ill. He was admitted to hospital and a gastro-enterotomy performed. This was a major operation, and one of the first of its kind. It involved cutting out part of the colon, then joining up the gap. Although the surgery was successful, Mother was told that Father's life was endangered. The operation had left him very debilitated. He might only survive a few years. He needed a long rest.

Mother's courage and practical sense was mobilised. She gave up the house in Lime Grove, rented a small cottage in Surrey, near Horsley Station, and took the whole family to the country. With three small children, a delicate husband and none of the amenities and conveniences of a London house, life must have been hard for her. The nagging anxiety over dwindling savings and Father's ill-health must have been appalling but I remember Mother as always energetic and cheerful, coping with each situation with ingenuity and humour.

I can still picture the cottage vividly. At the end of the garden was a bank of daffodils in full bloom. The architecture and the interior of the cottage leave but a faint trace on my inward eye but, among other vivid and indelible mental pictures is the railway cutting with its wild flowers, especially the large daisies which I picked for my teacher. Remembered scenes of walking through fields and climbing over stiles on my way to the village school with the station master's daughter, bring back a happy memory of a much-loved companion who was just old enough to look after me. Later, as Father gradually got better he resumed work and we, the original Railway Children, would wave to him as he climbed the station steps to the platform.

To have Father well again and earning a living for the family was wonderful. He ignored the doctor's prognostications and lived on into his seventies. His illness and delicate health became useful tools with which he dominated my mother, who spent the rest of their married life ministering to his every need.

Shortly after Father's recovery we moved to a house in Shoot Up Hill, North West London. Shoot Up Hill is part of a Roman road which stretches from Marble Arch to Edgware, connecting the shopping streets of Kilburn High Road and Cricklewood Broadway. Just on the edge of London's growing urban sprawl, the location delivered many rural delights and real country was not far away. Trams ran outside our door and there were special, never-to-be-forgotten expeditions.

Father would often take me out on Sunday mornings, while Mother was busy with the babies and the preparation of Sunday dinner. The tram terminus was at Canon's Park, where buttercups, dog daisies and myriad rustling grasses grew shoulder high. Memorable mornings consisted of a bunch of flowers clutched in one hot, sticky hand, the other clasped in Father's, with the rapture of the meadows enhanced by the company of the dearest person in my world. Near our house there was a 'Home of Rest for Horses' and country walks full of interest. One particular cinder path was regularly trodden in delightful anticipation, small gifts of carrots and apples for the aging horses in their 'Home of Rest' in Cricklewood Lane and for the animals at Dicker's Farm, carried in a crumpled paper bag. Sadly, all that now remains of that thrilling childhood destination is the name Farm Avenue. Suburban houses have long since swallowed up the fields, trams no longer shuttle pilgrims to paradise, and Canon's Park is unrecognisable as the real country of my memories.

Hampstead Heath, thankfully, remains its dear self. A short walk along Mill Lane, Fortune Green Road and Platts Lane or Heath Drive would bring us to its borders, the heath rising green and vast before us. Most of this walk is still unchanged and my children and grandchildren have shared the same simple joys of feeding the ducks, sailing model boats, climbing trees and, in winter, tobogganning down the hill which I can still see now from the window of my present home.

Before the First World War, most of the houses radiating out of London into the suburbs were inhabited by single families. Our house in Shoot Up Hill was considered scarcely adequate for an ordinary family with three children and a maid. Later there was either a nanny or a governess as well.

On the ground floor there was a drawing room, dining room, kitchen and 'morning room'. Upstairs were bedrooms for my parents and my brother and one which my sister and I shared with the governess or nanny. One of our nannies, instead of making the nocturnal crossing of the landing to the lavatory, used a chamber pot in the bedroom. This was a source of endless hilarity to my sister and me, supposedly asleep but in fact wide awake to the event. Onomatopoeic rhymes, with a chorus of piss percussion and fart horns, became secret hysterical jokes. Next to our room, there was a small room for the maid and, down three magic steps, the nursery. Father once fixed a board over the stairs so that we could slide down into our childish kingdom. In the front garden stood a monkey puzzle tree, our spiky guardian angel. It is still there.

The house comprised nine rooms, plus bathroom and toilet, and accommodated six, sometimes seven, people. It was not unusual in most of these suburban homes to find at least two maids, one to help with the housework and one with the children. Other people, such as a gardener or a sewing lady, came at odd times. And yet mothers were not idle. Cleaning, cooking, washing, ironing, mending, preserving fruit and vegetables, making jam and entertaining; all involved enormous and unremitting toil without the benefit of electricity or detergents.

Pea soup fog and smoky chimneys deposited layers of sooty dust that had to be removed daily. Vast quantities of soap, soda, Monkey brand, hearthstone and blacklead were applied with what Mother called "elbow grease". In the drawing room, armchairs were covered with loose chintz covers which children helped to remove when guests were expected. Household jobs left hideous scum around sinks and bowls which all had to be thoroughly scoured. Wooden tables and draining boards were all scrubbed white. Carpets and rugs were hung out on the clothes line and beaten with cane beaters, which are now sold, along with other common household utensils of those days, as antiques. Women's muscle power was the main source of energy and it was in plentiful supply and cheap or free. No energy crisis was even dreamed of.

Fifty years later, as a member of the Camden Council Social Services Committee, I had occasion to return to Shoot Up Hill. We had purchased two houses there to use as Children's Homes. As I approached one of the houses I saw that it was not far from our former family home. A few doors down, the monkey puzzle seemed to nod in faint remembrance.

The Council house had been splendidly converted for its purpose but I was struck by how much ideas about living space had changed during the half century that spanned two world wars. A house considered too small for our family had been converted into living accommodation for twice as many people: twelve children and two members of staff. Two double bunks would easily sleep four children in each bedroom. As I stood there, I thought back to when our family had first moved into the nearby house. We had to wait some time for our bedroom furniture to arrive and Mother, never at a loss in any household emergency, put us children to sleep in the kitchen dresser drawers! Nowadays kitchen drawers would never be large enough to comfortably hold a four-year old child.

In fact, it seems to me that everything has shrunk: families and their communities, the houses in which they live, the sacred invisible circle of concern and responsibility drawn about them. Although London family homes spread rapidly between the two world wars, space became more expensive and houses were built smaller. Most pre-war houses are now shared, converted into flats or bed-sits. Many families occupy only two or three rooms, with a cooker on the landing, shared toilets and bath or perhaps no bath at all. In the inner London area there are still homes to be found with only outside lavatories, in spite of colossal building programmes. Households have also become more concentrated, not only because couples are having fewer children but also because labour-saving devices and social reform have led to profound changes in the way English society operates. The vast army of maids, nannies, governesses, gardeners, maiden aunts and other distant relatives who used to help in the home in exchange for low wages or merely board and lodging, has been silently, subtly decommissioned.

Heaven knows, I rejoice in social justice, but how I mourn the loss of those extended families. Now widowed and in my ninth decade, I know so many people who live alone, existing on ready-made meals heated up in the microwave. I can't believe that this lifestyle is a healthy one. Nutrition is one thing but we also need to nurture and be nurtured, to play our part in a caring, connected society, to hang on for dear life to the human factor.

When I was a child I used to be surrounded by people. Entertaining was frequent. The house always seemed to be full of uncles, aunts and cousins who would drop in at any time, always expecting to stay for a meal or overnight. Mother would keep her store cupboard well-stocked with good things which would "come in handy" for these impromptu visits. Relatives would invariably appear on Sundays to sample our wine and Mother's home-made cake. For an overnighter, we children would be bundled together. There could be up to five children in one bed, sleeping in a space-saving top-and-tail arrangement, one child's feet towards the next child's head. I don't think they ever let boys and girls sleep together, however, unless they were very small.

My mother, like her mother before her, wanted to run a proper orthodox Jewish home. Whenever I challenged this, she would say it was because Grandmother Silverstone insisted. My grandmother was a very strong character, partly by nature, partly because circumstances had made her so. . Her eldest son, my Uncle Will (who had a wooden leg due to the Boer War), fell in love with a girl called Rose. Rose was very English, very working class, and Will absolutely insisted on marrying her. My grandmother was extremely upset about this but Will was adamant. Rather than lose her son, Grandmother Silverstone insisted that Rose should come and live with the family for six months and learn how to be Jewish. Rose complied with this wish and was eventually converted. I can't help thinking of how a friend of mine, who also converted to Judaism, once described the Jewish religion as a food parcel; all her future mother-in-law would talk about was food, which is very often the case. I wonder what Rose had to go through before she and Will married and moved to Southend. They did very un-Jewish things like running a whelk stall on the sea

My mother

front and taking in lodgers for the summer holidays. They had six children who were all extremely beautiful. Three married Jews and three married non-Jews but they were all very much part of our family circle. My grandmother must have been unusually enlightened. Many similar families would have rejected the young intermarried couple and mourned the son as if dead.

I did not share my mother's trait of unquestioning obedience. I was the horrid child who always wanted to know the whys and wherefores of everything. Father was always more prepared to discuss things but he was a bit of a hypocrite in many ways. Jewishness centred around food and Father insisted on having a Kosher home. This meant that you didn't eat milk with meat and had to wash up eating utensils separately, that you had special food for Passover, candles on Friday night and lots of things that are important in a Jewish home. Yet Father would go out to restaurants and tuck in to oysters, lobsters and other forbidden foods.

I remember my first transgression of the Jewish culinary code. I was with some naughty cousins in the East End during Passover and we bought some sweets and ate them. We didn't fall down dead, in fact nothing happened at all. So, I thought, God *doesn't* punish you for eating sweets in Passover. My faith took a hard knock that day!

The Passover is, of course, 'The Last Supper' of the New Testament. The festival lasts a whole week starting with the meal and the blessing over wine and motze, which is unleavened bread, like water biscuits, to remind you of the hasty departure of Jewish slaves from Egypt, giving no time for bread to rise. During the meal, bitter herbs recall the bitter life of slavery; a mixture of grated apples and almonds symbolises the missing cement in the building of possibly pyramids with heavy stones. The youngest child asks set questions and the father of the house tells the story of slavery and God's gift of deliverance and freedom, a story repeated over and over through six thousand years of Jewish history and never ending. The week-long festival is preceded by a thorough cleansing of the house and all utensils used for food. Most orthodox homes have special sets of crockery, cutlery and cooking utensils only used during Passover.

Once my sister Sally and I had gone on some expedition or other and come into the possession of ham sandwiches. The pig was a forbidden food as it is in the Muslim religion, perhaps because it was considered unhealthy. Many rules about food seem to have connection with health. Over the ages the Jewish sages spent hours and hours in endless discussions over the meaning of phrases in the Bible such as "Thou shalt not seethe a kid in its mother's milk", which led to strict rules about keeping dairy produce and meat separate. Some Jews even have separate sinks and pots and pans for milk dishes or meat dishes, always eaten at different meals. Reform or Liberal Jews, in the words of a Rabbi I knew, believe that God is not interested in pots and pans or dietary laws!

We ate the ham sandwiches in great trepidation. Sally was promptly sick but I enjoyed them, so my faith disappeared for ever. What child can resist secrets or the breaking of taboos, and the guilty excitement of forbidden knowledge and wicked words?

I was taught that God would punish me if I were sinful and I remember that a pimple on your tongue meant God was punishing you because you had told lies. If you had bruises on your body that you could not account for, that too was a punishment that had come from God. So God was all mixed up with my mother's threats and punishments. I used to recite the 23rd psalm when fearful that I would be punished for wrongdoing.

Our family kept all the Jewish festivals. We had to go to the Synagogue every Saturday and to Sunday School, and we had a private Hebrew teacher some of the time. I was very jealous when my brother Phil had his Bar Mitzvah, which involved him being given wonderful presents and having a huge party in a restaurant on the Finchley Road. I thought it was outrageous but in those days no-one had ever heard of a girl having a Bar Mitzvah. Nowadays Jewish girls enjoy similar celebrations.

A Bar Mitzvah is a Confirmation ceremony. In the Synagogue a boy of thirteen comes of age, reads a portion of the Bible and promises to uphold the Faith and to be responsible for leading a good life according to God's Law. In more Liberal congregations girls may have a Bat Mitzvah.

We had a very busy social life. There always seemed to be a Jewish celebration, like a wedding or Bar Mitzvah, to go along to. These were excellent occasions for a party. Often there would be a huge dinner with a dance to follow in a hired hotel or hall.

In those days entertainments and amusements were all home-made. We children enjoyed the board games Ludo and Snakes and Ladders. We often played what is now called Bingo, but which then we called Lotto. My mother dealt the cards and a large bag of Cowrie shells, which we used to cover the numbers. Now it's a grown-up gambling game but in those days it was one of many family games. Other favourite games included quizzes, spelling games (forerunners of 'Scrabble'), charades, devising plays to surprise the grown-ups and endless practical jokes. When anyone came to stay, we delighted in making apple pie beds for them (doubling the bottom sheet so that one's legs could reach only half-way down) and sewing up the legs of their pyjamas. One night, some newly-wed cousins stayed and we put a reel of cotton in the chamber pot under their bed. The thin trail of cotton led from the chamber pot to the next room where it ended its journey in the hands of a child who would wind the cotton at intervals throughout the night. Imagine the consequences!

We did not have television or radio, or even a gramophone until after the First World War. Children were taught to recite, sing, dance or play a musical instrument in order to entertain guests. I was in disgrace when I angrily said, "Oh, Mother, don't show off your children". The girl next door would play the violin, as would one of my cousins, and I enjoyed playing accompaniments on the piano. My Uncle Alex could sing *Speak to me Thora*, which was a special favourite among the emotional Victorian songs, during which the ladies daintily mopped tears from their eyes with lace-edged handkerchiefs.

One day Father bought a gramophone and we children heard orchestral music for the first time – the *Zampa, Poet, Peasant* and *William Tell* overtures were never to be forgotten. *Ombra Mai Fu* and Handel's *Largo* were among those early records.

If we weren't playing parlour games, we were usually to be found outdoors, playing the games that all children play – tag and touch, mothers and fathers, skipping games, playing at schools or shops. We made up all sorts of games, as well as secret languages. In our suburban neighbourhood we had to stay in our garden and weren't allowed to play out in the street. We looked forward to visiting our relatives in the East End where we could chase each other round the streets and play wonderful games like hopscotch, marbles, cops and robbers and Knock Down Ginger. This last game was a delight to play in the narrow streets where there were no front gardens. We would tie a piece of string to the knockers of two front doors opposite each other, knock on each door, then run away and hide. Another good East End game was to lean out of a window, holding a long thread attached to a coin which we had left on the pavement. When a finder stooped to pick up the coin, it would be whisked away under his very nose.

We didn't have elaborate toys then as children have today. I never played with dolls, except for one special rag doll called Jimmy Noodle who was my constant bedtime companion. I envied Phil his toys and activities. He wore sensible clothes with lots of useful pockets, "Rubbish pockets!", Grandfather Goldbloom used to tease. Phil once carried around a dead mole for days – it was so soft! I, however, had no pockets; there was nowhere for me to store sweets, bits of string, stones, dead animals. I even had to tuck my handkerchief under the elastic of my knickers.

I did make some advance towards sexual equality, however, in the area of literature. Alongside the usual school stories, I read a lot of boys' books. I avidly read comics such as *The Magnet* and *Gem* and devoured my brother's adventure stories rather than those considered suitable for girls. I was, and still am, a voracious reader and loved books above all playthings. My sister Sally, by contrast, was happy with dolls. Her greatest delight was to be entrusted with babies or toddlers – the real live dolls. In our family, there was always a new baby cousin around to cosset and cuddle.

I started real school when I was five years old. I went to a small local private school. A board at the front of the building declared it as 'Wycombe House School for the daughters of gentlemen'. In those days a 'gentleman' was a man who drew his income from the property he owned and did not have to work for a living, but my father and all the other fathers were in trade or a profession.

We were not taught domestic skills at school, nor at home, because we had maids. My mother was, nevertheless, very active in the home. She did the cooking, with the maids bringing this, that and the other, chopping the vegetables, washing up and clearing away. A tremendous amount of sewing was also done at home, partly because my father was in the rag trade and he could bring home lots of remnants but also because it was the custom of the time.

A sewing lady used to come once a week. The sewing machine would be going and we would stand on the table to be measured or to try on the clothes. I can remember a Little Lord Fauntleroy suit, made of black velvet with a white lace collar and steel cut buttons, which Phil had for best.

Our school clothes were rather more prosaic. We girls used to wear gym tunics, a simple design based on wide shoulder straps attached to a yoke, fanning out into pleats. We wore them with braided belts, different colours often denoting which hockey team you belonged to, which form you were in, or some other scholarly significance. These home-made clothes were always made too big for us so that we did not grow out of them too quickly. Our navy serge knickers used to show below the gym tunic. The humiliation endured was terrible, not to mention the anxiety experienced at the thought that they might fall down. Elastic was not very good in those days. Women of my generation were brought up on the twin fears of our knickers falling down in the street or at a party and that we might get run over when wearing torn or dirty underwear. We were strictly forbidden to use pins instead of having our clothes properly mended, just in case we did have an accident.

We wore black stockings made of lisle, a sort of cottony stuff. We didn't have silk stockings until we were grown-up. In winter we wore a vest underneath, then combinations, which we hated. They were all-in-one affairs made of scratchy wool with long sleeves, buttons at the neck, legs reaching to the knees and a slit so that you could go to the loo easily. On top of these two garments came the Liberty bodice, made of knitted cotton reinforced with tape, and from that hung suspenders which fastened your stockings. On top of this came cotton knickers, then the navy blue serge ones. Next came a blouse, a tie and the gym tunic. At weekends, we used to exchange our school uniform for a petticoat and dress.

As for shoes, these were sensible lace-ups, but my mother once bought me some very fancy shoes made of black patent leather. They were as high as boots, with four straps and buttons around the ankle. How I hated wearing them and dreaded the thought that one of my school friends might see me.

Hair was very important. Long hair had to be worn either in plaits or tied back with a ribbon. My hair was a bright ginger colour, very curly and I was always teased about my unruly mop. There was a popular song of the day called "Ginger, you're barmy". Kids in the street used to call this out after me adding, with a modicum of inspiration, "Get your hair cut". My hair was not considered at all attractive until I was older.

I stayed in the all-female environment of Wycombe House until I was sixteen. I am, and shall remain, ever grateful to the English teacher who gave me a lasting and all-absorbing love of literature. I was tremendously interested in anything that was new, from Ethel M Dell to Michael Arlen. Books had a very great influence on my life. As a teenager I started to read French. Voltaire was a special favourite and I read Maupassant, Anatole France, Balzac. I devoured every new book.

Drawing, too, figured highly as a favourite occupation, so art lessons were eagerly awaited. In those days, classroom art was confined to copying and drawing neatly. I wanted to do so much more. I remember a reproduction of Watts' *Hope*, which depicted a sad lady sitting on top of the globe, playing a harp, which seemed an important thing in my life.

I also remember the Maths teacher, nick-named Smuts, very clearly. If you had done anything wrong she would call you out to the front of the class and, during the course of her admonishments, she would gradually push nearer and nearer to you, spitting as she spoke. Naturally, you would retreat from this shower of spittle, so that by the end of the talk from Smuts, you would find yourself with your back up against the classroom wall. But Smuts was a good teacher and I quite liked her lessons.

History and Geography were taught separately: the different periods of history; lists of kings, queens and war;, countries and their exports. I found all this very boring. Botany, on the other hand, I adored. We would go on botany rambles, gathering wild flowers to take back to the classroom where we would identify them, dissect them and draw them. These floral investigations, the naming of the parts and their functions, fed my abiding interest in sex and reproduction.

Friendships at school were all-important. Changing loves and hates caused jealousy and uncertainty. Quarrelling and bullying were daily events. Mother had many sayings and slogans and she would meet tearful accounts of fighting or cruelty with "You must fight your own battles".

It seems that is just what my brother Phil did. He often came home from school with torn clothes, a black eye or bruises, only to be chastised for fighting again. I found that girls were more subtle in their aggression. Like the boys, they formed into gangs, some more prestigious than others. Loners were the victims of tortures devised by gang leaders. Capturing a girl and surrounding her in the playground used to pass for fun, and terrorising her by putting live spiders down her neck was hilarious. Forcing her to lick a worm, to kneel and pray for mercy to strange invented gods, to submit to hair pulling, finger bending, arm twisting, anything that ended in tears, was a triumph. One girl who was bullied told her mother, who came to complain to the Headmistress. Unfortunately the mother was seen entering the school and the guilty gang sent the girl, the sneak, to Coventry for a week. How little anyone cared about her agony of loneliness and ostracism. When does compassion awaken in children? They seem to be cruel and sympathetic by turns, loving and then hating their contemporaries, adoring and tending their pets with loving care one moment then abandoning them casually, even teasing or ill-treating them. They can be alternately maternal or vicious towards younger brothers and sisters. Older ones always get the blame for bullying or provoking the youngsters, who know only too well how to get their revenge.

At home I was always being blamed for attacking Phil and Sally. How I enjoyed banging their heads together: a short-lived enjoyment, since they regularly ganged up against me and teased me. Childhood punishments were administered by the powerful triumvirate of Mother, Father and God. I was taught that if I were sinful, God would punish me. So God was all mixed up with corrective threats and punishments but, curiously, also with protection against punishment. In truth, my mother's threats were always worse than her actions but they engendered acute anxiety. She would, for instance, threaten to run away and leave her naughty children to fend for themselves. "Is Mother in?" were the first words we uttered on coming home after an outing or from school, words which always had a ring of doubt.

One of my most painful and humiliating childhood memories was of being sent down the road to a hardware shop to buy a penny cane. I remember whispering so quietly that the shopkeeper had to ask me to repeat the ghastly request over and over again. The crooked length of fine bamboo lay upon the table as a silent threat, but was in fact rarely used.

After school we had private lessons at home. We were tutored in piano, dancing, Hebrew and elocution – a correct accent was considered essential. Occasionally I went to concerts with my music teacher, the beginnings of a great interest in music. I later went alone to the Queen's Hall promenades and other concerts.

I was anxious to grow up. By the age of about twelve I had visions of myself as a beautiful, tall, willowy woman, wearing long skirts and a large hat anchored with hat pins to a pile of hair. Alas, like many of my dreams and ambitions, this was never to be realised. When I was old enough for adult fashions, both skirts and hair had been cropped short!

* * *

Change came soon enough. The 1914–18 war clouded family life, irreversibly dividing life into pre- and post-war periods. The pattern was repeated in 1939–45, when I was caring for my own children. Twice in my lifetime, both as a child and as a mother, wars wrought climactic changes, altered plans, re-directed thoughts, feelings and actions.

For Phil the war was exciting. His games and toys echoed the male aggressive theme. I, too, drew war pictures and made up silly rhymes echoing my mother's admonitions, especially about not wasting food. The Food Controller appeared as the bogey man to come and punish children who did not eat every crumb of scarce, rationed food placed before them. We had some revolting kind of margarine, which we'd never seen before. I don't remember being hungry but I do remember being made to eat horrible food and crying into hated rice pudding, served up again and again at different meals, until I finally swallowed it. To this day I cannot eat milk puddings!

I can remember Zepellins flying over the house. When there was an air raid warning we would be taken from our beds and brought down to the kitchen. We enjoyed hot cocoa sitting underneath the kitchen table. My father would go out to see what was happening while my mother screamed at him to come inside and take cover. One day a bit of shrapnel fell through the roof, and anti-aircraft guns actually brought down a Zepellin in North London, to our great excitement. After this my father decided that my Mother should take us away from London because of the danger. We went to live at Hove, in a flat over a shop, and my sister and brother and I went to school there for a few years during the war.

Our cousins, in uniform, seemed glamorous. An extremely beautiful cousin with blue eyes and golden hair tied back with a big black bow was my role model, a typical flapper. All the boys in uniform wanted to take her out. She never used make-up, as only 'fast' girls bought rouge and lipstick. Instead she reddened her lips with beetroot and rubbed 'papier poudre' on her face – tiny booklets of powdered paper were an innocent substitute and less reprehensible than a box of real powder and a puff.

Eventually the war was over. I was twelve in 1918 and I can remember sitting atop the garden gate waving a Union Jack. Children were growing up into adults. The word teenagers was never used and adolescence never mentioned. The majority of children became wage earners when they left school at fourteen.

Wartime memories are hazy but I don't remember ever feeling afraid or compassionate or horrified at the ghastly slaughter. Childlike, I took my cue from my parents who later taught me in my turn how to be calm and resourceful for the sake of children, who live in their own present and whose sufferings and joys have little to do with the great world outside home and school.

My brother and sister are dead, so I cannot check my memories against theirs. I feel sure that their impressions and feelings would be quite different, not only because neither had children, which changes perception of the past, but also because the view backwards changes according to experience, position in the family, interfamily relationships, friends and outside interests.

* * *

We children grew up, Father's business prospered, Mother moved up in the social circle and, eventually, persuaded Father to buy a larger house. We moved from No. 89 to No. 19 Shoot Up Hill.

It was utter bliss to have my own bedroom. My sister and I had grown to hate sharing a room. Our interests did not coincide and we had different friends. I could now surround myself with books and read late at night and early in the morning. There were other changes, too: a large garden with a tennis court, and a full-size billiard room for Father and his friends. No more soft gas lights with delicate lacy mantles and little chains for adjustment. There were electric lights in every room.

There was no longer a nursery with a coal fire and a fireguard upon which we would rest our feet while a paste made of Fuller's Earth dried on our chilblains. Now there was central heating or gas fires or anthracite stoves, but no-one who has ever slept in a bedroom with a coal fire can forget the intense delight in the play of shadows and light on the ceiling before tired eyes closed.

Beyond the tennis court were vegetable plots surrounded by espalier fruit trees. Father's favourite time was spring. Then he would come home from work to stroll round the garden before dinner, marvelling at the yearly miracle of snowdrop, crocus, daffodil and hyacinth forcing through the dead earth, and later inhaling the fleeting delicate scent of apple blossom.

Mother revelled in the garden produce which she bottled, preserved and stored in her large cupboard. Like the linen cupboard, all contents were listed inside the door. Each week, menus were planned and jars of jam, bottles of fruit, eggs which had wintered in liquid isinglass and other stores were measured out for the kitchen.

A larger house meant larger parties. Mother was happily climbing her social ladder. When Father bought a car, all the aunties bought long chiffon motoring veils, hoping to be invited for a drive on Sundays.

Mother often went out in the afternoons with her friend in her chauffeur-driven car. Most afternoons were given to pleasure in some form – a shopping expedition to the West End with an ice cream at Selfridges, tea and white iced walnut cake at Fullers in Regent Street, a matinee or a bridge party. Such events called for the ladies' smartest afternoon outfits, with hats and gloves and handbags carefully matched. Clothes, like household furnishings and ornaments, engendered competition and were a source of endless conversation.

Clothes for all occasions and all seasons involved shopping expeditions and repeated fitting sessions at the tailors or dressmakers. As days became colder, furs would come out of store and, as the children took the guests' fur coats and stoles from them, they giggled when mothballs rolled out!

Some afternoons were devoted to charity work such as the Linen League, at which the ladies made long, white, cotton, divided drawers for the elderly women in poor-law institutes, or fancy goods for charity bazaars. Powder puffs of fur or swansdown sewn into pretty handkerchieves were popular and flaunted openly – so far had ladies progressed from the discreet days of the flappers.

I grew to dislike my mother's friends with their smug faces and their plump, bejewelled fingers crawling over the bridge table. I resented having to take a hand when a fourth was needed at bridge or when I was expected to hand round tea or cakes.

I would escape by locking myself in the lavatory with a book. Not one of those women in their circumscribed cocoons, reflecting their husbands' incomes and status, could have shared the agonies and ecstasies of Ibsen, Strindberg, Pirandello, Proust or Voltaire. Shaw and Wells and socialist ideals were worlds away from the idle chatter about musical comedies, maids, menus, clothes, shopping and gossip.

With youth's intolerance I could not understand that these pleasure-loving women were compensating for the hardships of wartime. Food was now abundant and to be enjoyed by those who could afford it. Those with successful husbands rejoiced in their good fortune while bereaved women, widows or spinsters were struggling with a new world. In my mother's circle few women were well educated. Mother was convinced that men did not like clever girls and a university career was totally discouraged. I knew a very few women living alone or with a friend and making significant contributions to the world of scholarship, art, music or social work. Some were even doctors and lawyers. I admired them from a distance and sometimes imagined a life among the dreaming spires, the independence of a challenging career. Sometimes my brother and sister and I discussed running away. Most children indulge in fantasies about escape from home but only for Phil was it to become a reality.

It was not an unhappy home. The big cloud of Father's anger burst frequently enough but we learned to notice whether his eyes were blue or grey and kept out of his way. Grey eyes presaged anger and Mother would usually be the target. Often she dissolved into tears, wailing, "What have I done to deserve this?" She felt so strongly that she lived up to her image of the good wife and mother but how little that was appreciated by her family, whose needs were so varied and incomprehensible to her. Nevertheless, Father tried to make amends but only until the next outbreak. My brother and sister always tried to love and comfort Mother, though I was usually on Father's side – bound up with his point of view. I shared his impatience with Mother's rigidity of mind and shared his despair when Mother dismissed all intellectual speculation and flights of imagination as "a load of tripe".

My father's encouragement of my exploration into the worlds of art, music and literature increased family tension and I was torn between father's approval and mother's disparagement. To Phil and Sally I was insufferably arrogant and priggish.

Death was a familiar presence in most families. In large families some of the children died young and almost always at home. Grandparents died in their own beds or in the homes of the next generation, with loving relatives at the bedside. Schoolchildren were not considered too young to take turns sitting at the bedside of a dying grandmother – listening to the stertorous breathing and the final death rattle as the old people passed away.

I remember being infinitely moved when gazing at my grandmother's face, now beautiful and unlined, the lines of age and anxiety, work and worry, smoothed away. This experience was repeated later with less emotion when my mother's mother died.

* * *

My parents had strong feelings about the dangers of arousing sexual precocity, yet their preoccupations were guaranteed to produce the very thing they feared most. Our sex education was aided and abetted by our cousins. Dirty jokes and obscene doggerel were exchanged with glee. Several generations later the same stories and rhymes cause sniggers at school and parents' consternation. Surely not everybody forgets so quickly? One cousin insists that he learned all the facts of life from me. By the age of twelve my role as sex-educator was well-established. One night I asked a girl cousin what she was doing in bed to cause so much agitation. She said, "I'm making pictures": an apt description of the fantasy life that is perhaps more important than the masturbation.

The parts of the body between the legs were never mentioned by their correct names. Their functions were distinguished by numbers – one and two – and great attention was paid daily to them. "Have you been today?" was the important question, the negative answer producing a dose of Syrup of Figs. Repeated negatives resulted in the dreaded castor oil.

Masturbation, though never mentioned, was a most important matter to parents, who went to great lengths to ensure that the private parts of the body were never touched. Hands were placed outside the bedclothes and quickly removed or slapped if caught between the legs. I heard recently about a mother who told her little boy to stop touching his genitals. "Why?" asked the child. "Because it's not nice", said the mother. "Oh, but it is," replied the child.

Times have changed and now one may read books and see films or TV programmes describing masturbation and all forms of sexual gratification, heterosexual, homosexual or in groups. Dildos, vibrators, condoms and caps are freely advertised and discussed. A character in the musical *Hair* says to a boyfriend who invites her to come to bed with him: "No, thanks. I'd rather go home and do it to myself." Quite unthinkable on the stage twenty years ago when masturbation was never to be mentioned in public and unimaginable even to suggest its existence in a romantic musical. Yet is there less sexual misery, fear, guilt today? Is there really greater happiness and fulfilment in these enlightened times?

As I look back on my childhood, I now realise that one must address the mysteries of sex – which seem to colour every aspect of life and the quest for wholeness and meaning – in terms of gender as well as sexual relationships. Why, I wondered even as a child, was I treated differently from my brother? Why did my mother ask my father to deliver punishment when serious crimes had been committed? Whence this assumption of male dominance, superiority and authority? My father's weekend post-prandial naps had to be respected. We children must never make a noise when Dad was asleep. Why was Mother never able to take a rest during the day? Endlessly the questions came.

My nose was always in a book. Why was I never given Meccano sets like my brother or a box of scientific experiments or conjuring tricks? I envied his presents as they made all too clear the distinctions between us. Phil once caused an explosion in the greenhouse, shattering glass and starting a fire. He had been given a chemistry set for a birthday present and Mother had decreed that he was not to make a mess in the house. The greenhouse seemed a safe and suitable place for some experiments and the explosion was totally unexpected.

"Quick!", shouted Mother, "The greenhouse is on fire, fix the hose while I telephone for the fire brigade." There was wild excitement in the house. The children, wide-eyed, watched the fire engine arrive. The helmetted men unwound the great hose and speedily extinguished the fire on which the garden hose had made so little an impression.

Father's rage was beyond all imagination when he came home from work to discover the damage to his beloved grape vine. His potted plants were destroyed and the greenhouse itself a blackened ruin. Poor Phil was thrashed again – he was the sort of child whose every activity led to disaster.

Phil would ruefully recall as an adult many incidents when his childish pleasures caused destruction of some object valued by adults, who swiftly took revenge in the shape of physical punishment. Always in trouble, he soon accepted his fate as the naughty boy of the family, feeling he might as well "be hanged for a sheep as for a lamb". His role brought some compensations for the miserable fate which cast him as the bad character in contrast to the good girls, his sisters. How he hated me as the eldest and the goody-goody – Daddy's pet!

My younger sister was frequently Phil's ally, ganging up with him to provoke me. Mother adored Phil. He was a delightfully attractive child, with blue eyes and golden curls. One day I laughed when Mother cried as she cut Phil's curls and gave him a boyish hair style. More malicious laughter echoed in my memories when I recalled a picture of Phil, in his black velvet Little Lord Fauntleroy suit with lace collar and cut steel buttons, being dumped in a dustbin by a group of bullying cousins in the East End.

Phil came into his own at school. Naughty children are often popular. They dare to do the mischievous things that all the others would like to do. If they take punishments bravely they become heroes. I found an easier way to popularity. Afraid of being bullied or disliked, unwilling to risk punishment for flagrant rebellion, I assumed the role of clown and developed an exhibitionist streak. A highlight of my school career was the ability to frighten children. A friend would warn a newcomer that I was mad and might have fits and when least expected I would perform my crazy antics in the playground.

Girls and boys went to separate schools but large families of brothers and sisters and cousins ensured that most children found plenty of opportunities to learn about the opposite sex though at school fantasy and gossip about sex differences were accented with giggles and sniggers.

All three of us made friends easily and Mother was always willing to entertain unlimited numbers of children. Although close in age, however, our tastes and friends were very different. It is difficult to remember when sex differences and different gender expectations first became evident. I was jealous of both younger siblings as long as I can remember. But perhaps it became evident when at about age five I went to an all-girls school and a year or so later, Phil was sent to a boys' school. Life then seemed to be very different for boys and girls. We entered separate worlds, of lessons, friends, games, clothes, hobbies. True, we played family games together but to me we were not the same species.

Adolescent to Adult

Home is where one starts from.
As we grow older
The world becomes stranger,
The patterns more complicated
of dead and living.
T S Eliot

I was bright at school and used to get prizes at the end of term but I was lazy and bored and never did any work. I was always in trouble for reading under the desk. My mother discouraged me from studying and aiming at University, whereas this little private school thought I might be University material. So I took Matric. I can remember it so well. There's a place in Queen's Square (I think it's still there) called the College of Preceptors where I had to go to sit the exams. I failed in my best subject, which was Maths, and you had to pass all five subjects at the same time to gain a certificate. I didn't take the exam again.

I was sixteen and very shy and inhibited and there were no boys at school. I had never been out with a boy except my cousins and my brother's friends in groups. I had played games and tennis with them but we were still children and sexual excitement or romance led only to giggles and secrets. I was all dressed up, walking in Queen's Square, and crowds of youngsters were milling around waiting to go in to sit the exam. Boys were there watching the girls. I was on my own, marching along, and went smack over onto my face! I was always very clumsy and stupid. The boys merely laughed. This might have been the reason for my failure!

My father made up his mind that I was going into the family business. In our set most girls didn't go out to work. We had a chauffeur and maids and my mother felt girls could spend their time arranging flowers, entertaining, learning such accomplishments as music and elocution, going to matinees and playing tennis. But my father believed in work, hated laziness and used to get quite angry if we stayed in bed in the morning. He had a puritanical streak where children were concerned. He wanted us to know the value of money and gave us good pocket money but stipulated what we had to buy with it. He encouraged independence in the management of money.

After I left school I went to a business training year at Regent Street Polytechnic. We learnt subjects such as commercial law and the Sale of Goods Act and studied commercial French and German. We had separate days for typing and shorthand. I always played truant and went to matinees, saving up my pocket money which was meant to pay for lunches and fares and so forth. We could go and have cheap meals at Lyons' tea shops, like beans on toast for sixpence, instead of going to the canteen at the Polytechnic.

I had a lot of fun there because in the lunch hour they had dances. There were boys and I danced with boys for the first time. My figure was quite good and slim. I was not pretty but had bright red curly hair and I was always known as "the girl with the red hair". I was mercilessly teased about my hair but at least I was noticed! Nobody fell in love with me, however, and I didn't fall in love. I was very backward and inhibited. I didn't menstruate until I was seventeen. My worried parents took me to the doctor who said there was nothing to be concerned about and I would probably menstruate in due course. I was different from everyone else and immature in many ways. I think my father had this fear of premature sexuality, or of children being sexual at all. If a boy had asked me to go out, I wouldn't have been allowed to go.

I remember later sitting out at a dance and a boy saying, "I brought you out here to kiss you and all you do is talk about Karl Marx!" Another boy said, "Talking to you, one thinks you are ready to go off to Paris for the weekend, but you won't even kiss." I was precocious mentally but backward physically.

I read everything. I got a copy of James Joyce's *Ulysses* in Paris when it first came out. I read in French, including the novels of Marcel Proust. Freud, Marx, Engels, Shaw and Wells were my idols. My father used to buy me the books. He was entirely self-educated and had very good taste. He was artistic and loved music. I had an aptitude for languages; my French was very good and later I learnt quite a lot of German as well.

Tallulah Bankhead was my favourite actress and Noel Coward was a must! The Everyman at Hampstead was then a theatre and I saw the MacDonagh players there with Esme Percy. Shaw, Pirandello, Strindberg, Ibsen – their plays were considered very avant garde in those days. I remember going with a girl friend once and we were so moved by something that we crawled down under our seats to hide our hysterical laughing and crying. I was always carried away by new ideas and always seeking a new philosophy of living. Every new author I read presented a new gospel.

In 1923, attending the Polytechnic, I would have worn little knee-length sleeveless dresses I had made myself with a yard of material from my father. Later I wore tailored suits which entailed several fittings. I wore a cloche hat and carried a handbag which always matched my outfit. I can remember around that time having my hair cut and shingled to the fury of my parents who were so upset and angry that it took a long time for them to forgive me.

In the evening I would be with my friends, trying on clothes, doing our hair and playing with make-up, which was permissible unless you plastered it on – something which was considered very common!

Then I was seventeen, coming up to eighteen, and felt very grown up. My father had made up his mind that I should work for him and I was so dominated by him that, although I had vague ideas of being an artist or a musician, I knew I was destined for the family business.

* * *

I was 'in business' with my father for about ten years and he trained me to be his right-hand man, or should I say right-hand woman? He used to lose his temper easily and when he shouted at me I'd go away and eat a bar of chocolate. I have a vivid memory of one day when he was in a rage, screaming at me. I looked at him and said, "You're behaving like a child." He went white and he walked away. I felt terrible. How could I do this to my father? Yet I realised my own strength and it frightened me.

My father didn't have a factory but, instead, as far back as I can remember, a West End showroom. He employed outworkers who had their factories in the East End, many of them sweat shops. In our showroom and workrooms we would have the cloth, linings and buttons, and so on. The tailors would come up from the East End with a large black linen cloth, make a bundle of all the materials and take it back to the East End by bus (by then there were motor buses as the horse buses had just about gone). In the workshop they would cut and make the coats and suits and bring them back and then we would pay them so much per garment. We would beat them down and get it as cheaply as possible and, accordingly, they would pay their workers as little as possible. If we didn't give the tailors any work they would sack the machinists, pressers, basters and cutters. All these people were only taken on when there was work. So there was terrible hardship and, as I got to know about this, I was very sympathetic with the garment-makers' unions which were becoming active in those days.

At first I was given the humblest jobs. I had to run out and do errands and buy cups of coffee or trays of food from a neighbouring restaurant for superior workers. As a 'matching girl' I was the lowest form of life. Silks and materials came wrapped in cardboard which were cut into strips with patterns of cloth pinned on. I had to go round to the various wholesale stores and get patterns to match the lining, or braid, buttons and buckles; all sorts of trimmings were used in those days. I would queue up and collect patterns, and come back with a whole lot of samples attached to the matching cloth. Somebody more important would then choose and order so many yards of this, that and the other, and a number of buttons, buckles, braid and other trimmings to add to the tailors' bundles.

My father trained me to be sociable and to be polite to customers. We would often entertain customers at home and sometimes I would take them out to lunch or tea. My father would cultivate the sales girls in the stores, hoping they would become buyers. We employed beautiful sales girls and models and showed the collections each season.

My father travelled a great deal, taking the models with him. They helped him pack and unpack the clothes and show them to customers in hotels all round the country. The garments were packed in layers of tissue paper in large baskets called 'skips'. Porters loaded and unloaded them onto hand trollies which they pushed between hotels and railway stations. Surrounded by lovely mannequins and sales ladies there must have been many temptations but I was

One of my illustrations in an invitation brochure for Thompson Goldblooms' autumn collection

grievously shocked when I finally found out about father's various sexual adventures. I never told my mother.

Occasionally, when a model was ill or away, I would accompany my father on his travels, packing and unpacking and modelling the clothes. Sometimes my father would send me into a store where, trembling with fear and shyness, I had to ask to see the buyer. Usually this request was refused but occasionally with rare good fortune, this important man or woman might deign to see me and – joy of joys! – accept an invitation to view the collection.

As well as working for Father three days a week I went to St John's Wood Art School for two days a week, where I would draw from plaster casts as well as from the nude. Mother was absolutely shocked. She could not believe that there were classes where boys and girls worked together from a nude model. The male models always wore little slips in those days but the women were totally nude. Nowadays even male models are nude. Being an art student, although only part-time, was heaven. I loved drawing, making friends and going to the dances and parties and 'rags'. But I was always terribly shy, very inhibited, and if anybody looked at me I would blush scarlet.

As part of my training my father took me to Paris and these were wonderful times. In those days going to the Paris fashion shows was exciting because buyers were welcomed with champagne parties and a special *vendeuse* treated one with ceremony, even if one bought only one or two of the models. My father would often buy the models to fit me and then we would copy them. In Paris, too, we would go to all the fashionable places, to the races, theatres and tea at the Ritz, to see what wealthy ladies were wearing. I would come back and do a whole bookful of sketches. I trained my eye to remember everything I had seen all day and then late at night I'd be sketching, sketching, sketching. Daddy would tear up the ones he didn't want, keeping suitable ones and details from others. We would go to the shows of Poiret, Schiaparelli, Patou, Chanel – all the leading houses. We also bought 'Toiles', models made up in a cheap cotton fabric to be copied.

We were always on the look-out for new designs, materials and trimmings and would collect addresses of suppliers in Paris. How we walked, indefatigably, along the Boulevards and into courtyards, climbing endless flights of stairs. There seemed to be very few lifts in those days and the ones we found were hair-raisingly rickety. One source of addresses was a 'Mr Plentylove' (called that because he was always talking about *l'amour*) who came to our London showrooms fairly frequently as an agent for various suppliers. Through him, we added to our list of firms to visit in Paris.

One day we called at an attractive showroom which had cupboards all round the walls and a carpet and curtains in attractive colours and patterns. Madame asked what we wanted and I said we were looking for model coats, suits, dresses. "Mais non," she said. I went through our list of materials: lace, braid, belts and so forth. At each request she shook her head. In desperation I said, "Mais qu'est ce que vous avez?" and she replied, "Nous avons des petites dames!" I took my father's hand and said, "Come on – this is no place for us." Unperturbed, she presented us each with her card, implying that she could cater to my sexual needs as well as Dad's.

At this time we still lived in Shoot Up Hill. My father had a car and chauffeur to take him to work but because I was always bad at getting up in the morning, he wouldn't wait for me. I would go down to Kilburn & Brondesbury station and go by the Metropolitan Line. There was a motive. Boyfriends would be on the train. It was part of my social life! We changed at Baker Street for Oxford Circus. At weekends we went north to 'Metroland' for picnics and country walks.

* * *

There's a story about my first dance! My friend who was over a year older had a Coming Out dance, and she invited me but insisted I put my hair up. She would not stand for kids at her party! My parents said, "Oh no! You're not eighteen and you can't put your hair up. If they won't have you with your hair down, you can't go to the dance." I cried and made a fuss, but they were adamant. So I went to the party with my hair tucked into my cloak hood and with a packet of hair pins in my pocket. When I got there I put my hair up somehow but the pins kept falling out. As I came down the stairs, one of the boys said, "Oh look! Rosie's got her hair up!" and started teasing me in front of everyone. I blushed scarlet – I was always blushing – it was shameful! We had little programmes with a pencil and each girl thought, "Oh, my God! I do hope my programme gets filled up!" Well, this time it did and I had the supper dance and the last waltz. That was terribly important because the last partner would probably offer to see you home and maybe ask you to go out. Nothing like this had happened to me before. I was having a wonderful time, apart from my hair falling down.

I went in to supper with a man called George. It all came back to me recently because he was buried on the same day as Mark. At the funeral I noticed his name outside the Chapel at the Crematorium. I hadn't seen him for about fifty years. How extraordinary to remember these things at my husband's funeral when I was in such a state of confusion and pain. I pictured a small supper table and my portion of Chaudfroid of Chicken. I remember starting to cut this chicken and it slid off my plate onto the floor. George bent down after it, calling out, "cluck! cluck! cluck!" I was desperately embarrassed and not amused at all. I wished I could sink through the floor and take the chicken with me.

At this dance I met two brothers and they offered to take me to a charity dance. I was dressed to kill waiting for them to call for me. When they arrived Mother said, "Oh, it's so good of you to take Rosie to a dance! She's never been to a big dance like that before!" I could have killed her. I was pretending to be so sophisticated, as if I went out to a dance every night of my life.

Later on there were lots of parties. We weren't in the class which was presented at Court, although we knew some people who were and who might have presented us. My mother and father thought being presented would give us ideas and we might then marry people who were not Jewish. That was always at the back of their minds.

Every year we had two huge parties, together with many small ones. We had a 'Bores' night which would be all the people we had to ask and then another night with all the people we really wanted. We had a billiard table which would be removed for the night. My mother was a wonderful housekeeper. If we brought half a dozen people home for a meal after tennis we could always be certain of Mother's hospitality. It was a very sociable life.

My father always played billiards or cards. In my whole life I can't remember my parents ever sitting at home alone. My father smoked cigars and my mother was a chain smoker. "I don't inhale", she would announce. Poor dear, she died of cancer but so did all her sisters who didn't smoke. I never smoked; I wouldn't do anything my mother did.

As time went on I had lots of boyfriends. There was always bridge, billiards, tennis. We would go to Neasden to the Tennis Club. Some of us formed a little private tennis club. We would hire a court and play in the winter at the weekend. I was always influenced by other people. I had a girl friend called Molly and she would get me up early in the morning to play tennis. There were two boys: Douglas Lyons who had an Austin 7 car and Harry Isaacs. They were my closest friends. We'd collect another girl and often go out together.

Westgate on Sea, 1928:
Douglas Lyons and Harry Isaacs awaiting a sensible response from Sally and me

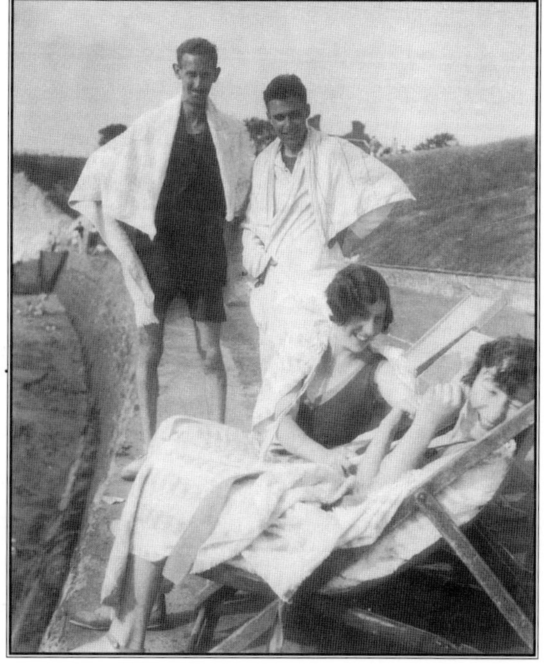

Typically, one night a group of boys and girls were at my house and we all wanted to go out but no-one had any money. We sat around and sat around and, in the end, we sat around all night and eventually went to the kitchen and made breakfast! When we were out we never wanted to go home, so we would go to one of the all-night street coffee stalls. If we had any money we would go to the Criterion for breakfast. The boys would pay for the girls.

Although I had a lot of boyfriends, none of them ever suggested going to bed with me. They would never have dreamt of such a thing; we hardly even kissed! In my mind I wanted to lose my virginity but in practice I could not bear to be touched. People kept proposing to me but I wasn't in love with them. I thought it had to be all or nothing, that I would fall madly in love and live happily ever after. It never occurred to me that I would want sex with anyone unless marriage was a possibility. Then I fell madly in love at first sight with a man I happened to meet at a dance. I was twenty. Harold came over and asked me to dance. I was thrilled and we danced a couple of times. Then I gave a dance and invited him. That's how it began. He had a friend and I had a friend and we started going out in a foursome. That was the great love of my life. It was all very slow and leisurely. We didn't even pet or anything. Once, trying to kiss me, he said, "You're very inexperienced!" I could have said, "So are you!" Instead I said he could teach me, but he never did!

Harold was very poor but he seemed everything I wanted. He was quite tall, with a big nose, and his clothes were shabby. He had a terrific sense of humour and played jazz on the piano extremely well. He danced well and was very well read. He was a doctor and wanted to be a psychiatrist. It was just beginning to be the 'in thing'. It wasn't even called psychiatry then but neurology. It was love at first sight although I knew nothing about him! I just thought, "There's a man I'd like to marry!" So we got secretly engaged. I don't think he was as serious as I was because he ended up jilting me. We had been going out together for over a year and had told some very good friends about our secret engagement. They invited us both to dinner for a celebration before we told anyone else. He didn't turn up. Imagine my feelings!

I insisted on seeing him and talking it over. We had a few sad farewell meetings. I even said I would go to bed with him but he refused. The problem was money. Harold had made up his mind to be a specialist. In those days, if you were a doctor, you had to buy a practice or you had to work for nothing in a hospital with a successful consultant who would gradually send you patients. So you could not possibly be a Harley Street specialist without money. There was no such thing as a paid hospital consultant: they were all voluntary in the hospital and made their money in private practice. You either had to have money or marry money. If Harold had intended to be a general practitioner my father could have helped to put up the money to buy him a practice, but not to keep him in the hope of getting to Harley Street.

His first job was a living-in situation in an institution on Harrow Road, run under the 'Poor Law'. It was a workhouse for poor and homeless families. Men, women, children and babies were all housed separately. There were staff rooms for single doctors only, with no room for wives or families. If we had married he would have been sacked. A colleague of his had been engaged for ten years with little hope of marriage but Harold would not contemplate such a fate for us.

There was a garden around this institution with a tennis court for the use of the staff. One sunny Sunday, wearing a short white dress and swinging my racket as I strolled with Harold and friends to the courts, a small red-haired child came running towards me clasping my knees and shouting, "Mummy, Mummy!". That was an embarrassment I never lived down!

I have never forgotten those intense feelings of first love – perhaps all the stronger for being unconsummated. That was the ideal against which all real experience was measured and found wanting. In Marriage Guidance the gap between fantasy and reality is often the source of unhappiness and estrangement.

Harold's mother was widowed. She was very poor and he was also supporting his brother to go through medical school. My brother and sister used to laugh at his shabby clothes and tease me. I think that one of the things that attracted me to him was that he was poor and making his own way, like my father. I like people who know what it is to be poor. So I was heartbroken over Harold who married late in life, was divorced and married again. He may still be alive. We didn't see each other again. I talked to him once on the phone when I was on the Greater London Council, about mental hospitals.

There was another doctor whom I liked very much and would have married, but he said to me very clearly, "I'm not going to marry until I'm forty, because I've got my career mapped out and I am going to be a specialist". And he kept his plan, although his parents could have supported him. Another wanted to marry me but tried to find out how much money I would have before proposing. I was disgusted!

I had lots of boyfriends and every time they proposed to me I said, "I can't ever marry because I love another. If I can't have him, I won't have anybody else." This was my role; I was playing this part. It kept me from getting emotionally involved but really I was scared of sex. There was a book at that time called *A Hard-Boiled Virgin* and I bought it, thinking, "That's me!" So there I was, having a good time because there were lots of parties, lots of boys, and there was the broken heart, and it was OK because I was safe. My parents were always urging me to marry this one and that one but I wasn't attracted. They weren't upset about the doctor because he wasn't good enough, because he was poor.

Holidays were always with my parents. Early on we went to the seaside where my mother would rent a house or flat and do all the catering, at Birchington, Herne Bay, Margate and so on. Later they would take us to hotels. For the Passover, the great place to go was Bournemouth, where there were several Jewish hotels. It was a recognised thing that whole families would come with their marriageable children and all the eligible young men would go to these hotels for Passover. They would have the service the first night and then the other nights there would be dances.

Everyone was looking for eligible partners. Girls and their mothers spent hours and hours matching shoes, gloves, handbag and hat to their dresses. If you had several outfits, everything had to match, and that took a lot of time. As a working girl I could pop out in the lunch hour. I had about the same amount in wages as my non-working friends were given pocket money. I learnt to be very quick about shopping. And hats? Oh, hats! We used to buy hats in Curzon Street in Mayfair. Hats were important. For example, when you went to a tea dance or were at a garden party, you wore a hat.

There were tennis and walks and golf and riding. You always picked up somebody in Bournemouth, often boys from the provinces. Once, when I was about twenty three or twenty four, Douglas and Harry and my sister and I went to stay at a Jewish hotel without my parents. That was allowed.

Sons and daughters were dominated by parents, even when working, and usually stayed at home until they married. Even at the age of twenty one, as a young working woman earning her own money, I felt the parental oppression that refused all freedom to unmarried girls living at home.

At eighteen I had fallen in love with the brother of the proprietor of a Jewish hotel. He was a regular Army officer, the last thing you would expect to find at a Jewish hotel at Passover! He was helping his brother while he was on leave before going out to India, and I fell madly in love with him. My family teased me by saying I had fallen in love with the waiter. He was forty and single and I was eighteen. Back in London he took me out to tea dances. We corresponded. He wanted me to go out to India. My father must have discussed this with my mother and told her not to say anything. One day he came to me and said, "You're getting yourself into a mess with that man. Don't you think you had better get yourself out of it?" That was all he said. I realised he was right. It was extraordinarily enlightened of him and it shows the kind of man my father was. I think he knew I would do anything he told me to but I realised myself that the affair was ridiculous. I was a Socialist even then and I couldn't imagine myself as an Army wife in India.

During the sad period after Harold jilted me, a girl friend suggested a skiing holiday. Both sets of parents were aghast at the idea. Two unmarried girls travelling abroad and staying unchaperoned at a hotel. This would doom them forever to spinsterhood. No-one would marry girls with the evil reputation that would ensue. Secretly we plotted and planned. My friend's brother and his friend had arranged a skiing holiday but refused point blank to be saddled with his sister and me. At last, after endless cajoling and persuasion, they agreed that we would travel and return together but that we would separate and rejoin at Chur to go separately to St Moritz and Arosa. The parents never discovered the deception. The older boys were acceptable as chaperons. We had the time of our lives and, although nobody seduced us, some English families at the hotel were quite shocked to find such nice girls unchaperoned.

By the time I was twenty four, I was 'on the shelf', an old maid. But I was working for my father and I had a wonderful time with him.

* * *

And what were Sally and Phil doing during this time? Sally spent a year at a finishing school in Switzerland and then joined me in the business. I especially followed Phil's escapades with both interest and envy. We were three siblings in one family, only just over a year apart in age, but worlds apart in experience!

My brother was in his teens when a very pretty maid seduced him. The pleasure was immeasurably enhanced by the knowledge that his silly sisters and censorious parents had no idea what was going on under their own roof. Secrets were fun, especially because of Mother's dictum: "Never have secrets from Mother!" Mother's slogans were reinforced by the image of God – a man up in the sky with an all-seeing eye, who was somehow in communication with parents so that they knew all the children's sins.

Phil knew this was nonsense and his crimes increased. He and his friends discovered girls who were quite different from their boring sisters good-time girls. You met them in the High Street or, if you could afford it, in the dance halls and night clubs that proliferated after the First World War. Further afield was the Palais de Danse, a flamboyant, noisy, elaborately-decorated place where you could pick up partners and practice the latest steps and where, for sixpence a dance, you could hire an expert dancer – male or female.

Sisters were not allowed to visit such dens of iniquity. They only went to parties in people's homes and were always chaperoned. At eighteen, aping the upper classes, they 'came out' at a private party and only after that would they be permitted to go out with a young man.

Long before that great age, Phil had learnt far more of real life than I would ever know, despite my secret reading of books that would have horrified my parents. The maid taught him to "be careful". She knew of girls who had been sacked when pregnant, even when the master or the son of the house was the father. Boys soon found out about French letters and dared each other to go into the barber's shop to buy a packet. Eventually, of course, Mother found them in Phil's pocket. She told Father and a really vicious thrashing resulted.

I talked endlessly about this to Phil, finding it hard to believe that he was really so experienced. Phil knew I was jealous of his daringness and his secret freedom. But fun could be bought. Nelly had told him about prostitutes who lived in Maida Vale with red curtains at their windows giving the signal that visitors were welcome, at a price. But such girls expected presents and the price of tickets for the dance hall or the back seats of the cinema (some cinemas even had double seats) had to be found somehow. Lack of pocket money led to stealing – mainly from Father but occasionally from Mother – and when this was discovered the reactions were painful and terrifying.

Thrashing was followed by copious admonitions, fiercely angry or tearful. A thief in the family! This was quite intolerable and an unbearable shock. When Mother said, "What would the neighbours think if they knew?" I immediately took Phil's part. I had a vivid sensation of horror. I was hurt beyond measure when I realised that the opinions of neighbours seemed more important to the adults than the family feelings that had caused such a catastrophe.

Poor Phil was always in trouble, yet only doing what many others did. In our rather divided family I was Father's pet. Mother, my sister and Phil formed another close little group. Phil was often odd-man-out, the naughty boy of the family, and Father was harsh and unjust with him. He was always picking on him and expecting more from him than was possible. If only Phil had been older, he might have been a war hero with a VC. Now, of course, some of the would-be heroes had returned though many had died. Among wounded relatives we knew of an artificial leg, a glass eye and other wounds which necessitated frequent stays at Roehampton. The children sometimes visited the "Men in Blue" there who were on crutches, bandaged, arms in slings. The horror and misery barely touched them at the time. Children take so much for granted. Empathy with the sufferings of others comes only with late adolescence, if at all. It is as if their own experiences are so crushing, so overwhelming, that the assimilation of personal events is more than enough. The facts of other people's lives are matters for curiosity often to be emulated or condemned. The child's world is black and white – goodies and baddies – and justice is the paramount virtue. "It isn't fair" is often on the lips of children yet they are rarely fair to each other.

Phil was envious of me as I was rarely in trouble. On my side, however, I envied Phil – he was a boy and thus was not afraid to take risks and dare to do things I only dreamt about. I was particularly jealous of his sexual freedom. To us adult sexual morality was absurd and hypocritical yet we could not break out of the straitjacket of the convention that ordained that girls should be virgins until marriage while boys might experiment freely with girls whom they would never marry. Still, the war did make a difference and some of our older cousins admitted that they could not possibly refuse the boys who were about to set off to the trenches.

If a girl became pregnant it had to be a secret. She was sent off to stay with an old nanny in the country and the baby was put into an orphanage. Girls who yielded were talked about and condemned. This was another aspect of parental behaviour that Phil and I found hard to forgive and one that brought the children together against the adults.

As far as my relationship with my brother and sister is concerned, I think I always resented them because of my very early feelings of deprivation. We were too close in age. They ganged up against me because I was the bossy one but they were very close with each other, sharing interests, ideas, work and friends. My brother was the naughty boy of the family, sandwiched between the two good girls, which must have been absolutely ghastly for him. He just couldn't do right in my father's eyes. He was nice looking, but my father preferred his 'good' girls. He used to beat Phil and I had this vision of his beautiful hands that were always threatening to hit somebody, although he rarely hit me.

I remember once Father did hit me on a very different occasion from the one mentioned at the beginning of this book. I can't remember what I had done, but he lost his temper with me. I can remember wearing a very pretty dress my mother had made. It was white with blue spots. My father went for me and, dodging out of his way, I tore this new dress

Father liked everything to look beautiful and to be just so. I can remember him coming in – probably after a very stressful day – and if the curtains weren't absolutely straight, he would grab them and pull them down.

He would get very angry with my mother and that I found most painful. He never hit her but he would shout at her and she would cry. I always sided with him, although I felt very guilty about that. I used to think, "well, really, she's such a fool, why can't she deal with him?"

When the time came for Phil to leave school and start work in the family business, he had to start at the bottom and learn the trade just as I had done. The glaring contrast between Father's indulgence towards me and his harsh fault-finding and bad temper with Phil was intolerable. Phil decided to run away. This had been the greatest secret of all – a plan shared by the three children and discussed for many years over clandestine midnight feasts or while smoking home-made cigarettes made from fag-ends, dried leaves and occasional stolen cigarettes, in the attic or at the end of the garden.

After all, many members of the family had run away. Before the war Uncle Sam, the cleverest and youngest of Dad's family, had won a scholarship to a grammar school, but he was teased because he was Jewish and had an East End accent and shabby clothes, so had simply disappeared when he was only fifteen. Three older brothers had emigrated. It was easy in those days to work a passage to the colonies. Sam joined his brothers in Australia but quarrelled with them and ran away again. Nobody knew his whereabouts. His parents and all the family became increasingly anxious, especially when the war started and spread and finally ended with still no news of him.

Imagine the excitement when Grandma suddenly received a letter ten years after his disappearance. Phil was most impressed; it was as romantic as any story we had read. How our school friends listened, mouths agape and eyes wide, to the real life story of Uncle Sam. His letter explained that he had decided not to write home until he had made good. After various travels and jobs he had joined the forces and fought through the war in Africa. At the end of the fighting he had taken advantage of the scholarships offered to ex-service men and was now a highly-qualified civil servant. As a colonial administrator he was entitled to six months' holiday in England every two and a half years, a reward for working in a gruelling climate.

When Uncle Sam actually came home on leave, the reality of his presence was even more thrilling than his letters. He was determined to give all his family a good time and even the children, his many nieces and nephews, received treats, outings and gifts. He seemed to excel in everything and especially shooting. There were many animal skins and horns distributed as proof of his prowess. In those days, far from being reprehensible, it was considered courageous to shoot wild animals. A tiger skin with a stuffed head became a favourite place for children to lie upon while reading or playing.

Why should Phil not follow in Uncle Sam's footsteps and eventually become a family hero? He promised to keep in touch with us and we swore never to divulge his whereabouts to our parents. When I was eighteen Phil disappeared from the family scene although he occasionally wrote to Sally and me. When he came home for my wedding he had been doing menial work in Canada and Australia and had many a tale to tell.

Déjeuner sur l'herbe, with members of the Goldbloom and Thompson families. From the left: my father, me, Philip, mother, Sally, Aunt Sadie

Marriage to Motherhood

Though even between the closest people
there persists infinite distances, a wonderful
living side by side can arise for them
if they succeed in loving the expanse
between them, which gives them the possibility
of seeing each other in whole shape and
before a great sky.
Rainer Maria Rilke

For a couple of years I enjoyed getting over my broken heart and then I began to tire of that role. Deep down there was an unhappiness at being at home, being single, working for my father and not having achieved anything career-wise. I wasn't an artist and I wasn't a musician. I thought, "Well, I'd better get over my broken heart, get married and get rid of my virginity." I decided, "The next person who proposes to me, who really attracts me sexually, I will marry." It happened to be Mark!

I met him at a tennis party and he suggested a return match. He then took me to the Aldershot Tattoo! He was good with boats and we had romantic times on the river. We had only known each other two or three months when he proposed and I agreed. When he started coming to the house, my mother said, "I don't know whether to be nice to him or not. Who is he? Who are his parents?"

Mark was the middle one of five children. His family was a little unusual because they were followers of Lily Montagu. She was a wealthy, unmarried Jewish woman who had started a settlement near Tottenham Court Road, where many Jewish families lived. She provided nurseries for babies and toddlers, clubs for mothers, teenagers and old people. She decided that she would be a Rabbi and built herself a synagogue. A Jewish female Rabbi was unheard of in those days, though with the development of the liberal and reform Jewish movements there are now women Rabbis. Miss Montagu attracted a large following and officiated at weddings and funerals in Mark's family as well as many others.

Mark's parents lived in Notting Hill, having moved from Soho. His father was a tailor, often out of work. His mother did sewing at home to scrape together a living for her five children. Mark was the brightest one and eligible for University but he refused a place because he decided to earn money to help the family. He had various jobs in the City and finally was offered free Articles to become an accountant. Most people had to pay to enter a profession, working full time and taking exams on the way. Eventually Mark and his best friend started up on their own and gradually built up a successful practice.

When we met Mark was thirty and I was twenty four. He was earning quite enough to get married, drawing about £1,000 a year, which was a good income then. It enabled us to have a maid and a car and later on a second car, and then a nanny as well as a maid. We lived extremely well. An average wage then was £1 or £2 a week.

Mark Hacker, in 1936 and aged 36

My father quite liked Mark and thought him a promising young man. We met in the summer of 1930 and after a few weeks were engaged and married in November. He seduced me before we were married. It was all done beautifully and gradually in the car or on a boat. He obviously went the right way about it. Under the watchful eyes of my parents, we never had the opportunity of spending a night together, so I lost my virginity in a car. Mark was very loving towards me, very sexy, witty and attractive. I knew that he had had a great deal of sexual experience and I felt very envious, but he was sensitive and skilled and sex was perhaps the best part of our life together. We decided that we weren't going to rely on French letters, now called condoms.

Because of my reading I sought a more modern method of birth control, the Grafenberg ring, which was rather like a modern IUD coil but in those days it was made of gold.

I decided to find a doctor who would fit the Grafenberg ring, which sounded easy but in reality was hard. I could not go to my family doctor – he wouldn't dream of helping me – so I had to find a woman doctor. I went along to one in the neighbourhood and she said, "Well, I hope you're a virgin. Come back to me after you're married." She didn't even examine me! I felt so intimidated that I didn't dare tell her I wasn't a virgin. I told Mark what had happened and he knew of a doctor who had helped him and his friends with abortions and birth control problems. I went to this doctor, who was most enlightened and understanding. He did not recommend the Grafenberg ring because of the risk of infection. Instead we talked about the available rubber things, either a Marie Stopes cervical cap or a diaphragm cap. I chose the Marie Stopes and and later changed to a diaphragm. I still think those devices are much better than the pill. Nowadays because of AIDS, in addition to the risks of unwanted children and venereal disease, people have so many more troubles over birth control, whereas the caps and condoms of my generation worked well (if you were careful enough), and without side effects.

When I married Mark I wore suitably off-white satin. With my Dutch cap in position I felt daringly modern! We had a real Jewish wedding. About five hundred people came to the reception at the Park Lane Hotel after the ceremony in Brondesbury Synagogue. We didn't want so much fuss but my father said, "I've given so many wedding presents, now you can get them all back!" My parents wanted a big party as our family had not had one since my brother's Bar Mitzvah. I still have many of the wedding presents even now.

Before the wedding we went house-hunting. We bought a house in Hampstead Garden Suburb, a fairly new concept designed by Canon Barnett and Dame Henrietta to provide a good life for all income groups working in London. Houses there were much sought after and it was very arty-crafty. People wore sandals and joined adult classes and it suited me fine! We had a car. Mark and three other chaps in the Garden Suburb went to work in an old banger, so I could have a car if I wished. But I walked a lot on the Heath and to Golders Green – there were then only two shops in the Market Place – and even to the fields beyond.

During the first ten years of my married life so many activities opened up that I'd never thought of doing before. Of course we continued to play bridge and golf and tennis, and we visited and entertained many friends. I joined an art class for sculpture and I joined the Workers' Education Association, the Labour Party and the Left Book Club, thus widening our circle of friends and acquaintances. After three years I became pregnant and no longer went out to work regularly and so was more involved with local activities. When I had a baby, I gave up work altogether.

I was almost leading two lives: the conventional, social Jewish life and at the same time I was going to classes and meetings and becoming political and trying to be worthy of my long-admired Suffragettes. (I can remember going to Trafalgar Square as a schoolgirl, hearing Mrs Despard and, overcome with enthusiasm, going up to her to kiss her hand.) The General Strike and the Hunger Marches had made me a Socialist and that was when I had started going alone to meetings and joining organisations, but now I had genuine colleagues and friends. Yet, while intellectually I inhabited a different world, my behaviour was still much that of my parents' world.

My father's business was on the top floor, on the corner of an alleyway off Oxford Street leading into Market Place. There was a little unheated turreted tower on one corner of our top floor which was where we kept fur trimmings. (It was not considered wrong to kill wild animals or wear fur in those days.)

From this little room with windows all round you could see along Oxford Street and it was from here that I first saw Hunger Marches in the Twenties and became aware of the English political scene.

The General Strike of 1926 was one of the many turning points in my life – a sort of key experience. I was very moved by all this and positioned myself totally on the side of the miners although the strike did not affect our little business. Many people were out to break the strike: there were students driving buses and everybody was giving people lifts to work. Public transport was at a standstill, with only a few buses being driven by students. It was rather fun, a kind of permission to be picked up by strangers in cars, which made for exciting adventures. That was the lighter side of it for me but underneath it all there was this dreadful awareness of people really experiencing hunger. I started to read a lot more about Socialism and I went to meetings, although I was not old enough or sufficiently politically aware to know a great deal about it, except that people were starving and that because times were bad mine owners had actually reduced wages. As a result, poor people couldn't manage and this went on all through into the Thirties. It was hearing one of the miners' leaders speaking that made me a Socialist.

I read Fabian tracts and books like Robert Tressell's *The Ragged Trousered Philanthropists.* I felt that man was on the way to being rational about life and that if everybody read Socialist propaganda, went to Fabian meetings and heard the miners' case, it would usher in a Utopian world of Socialism. I really believed that. A great many people like H G Wells, Bertrand Russell, George Bernard Shaw, G D H Cole, Harold Laski (one of my particular idols) and John Strachey were thinking and writing during the Thirties. Many years later Elizabeth Durbin, writing about her father, Evan Durbin, and his various colleagues, entitled her book *New Jerusalems,* reflecting Socialist thinking of that time. We always sang 'Jerusalem' at Socialist meetings. I was very shy but I would go to these meetings and sit at the back of the hall, not daring to talk to anyone. These were Fabian, Labour Party and sometimes even Communist Party meetings. My convictions became stronger all the time and I think the Fabian lectures had the most influence on me.

The Fabian Society was started by Beatrice and Sidney Webb and Bernard Shaw. It proclaimed 'the inevitability of gradualness' and its symbol is the tortoise. Fabians believe that no good comes though revolution; one must wait for education and majority decisions. I read Karl Marx and agreed that the workers were exploited and that profit and greed were not necessarily the only motivation for progress. Everything seemed so clear: there were people making too much money and most of those who had more than enough did not seem to care whether the poor had work or not, whether they had money or not, whether the children had shoes on their feet or enough to eat. I remember a time, after I was married, when the hated Means Test was operating. We were told of a poor family in Wales and sent them food parcels for quite a time. Finally, however, they asked us not to send them because the value of these parcels was deducted from whatever benefit they were entitled to. It was monstrous. I remember a teacher saying he couldn't teach the children in the Welsh mining valleys because they were so hungry, they needed food rather than lessons.

I had always done some kind of voluntary work in the East End, as did my mother and my grandmother. It's a Jewish tradition that, even if you're not very well off, you help the poor and do something to justify your existence. I did Care Committee work in the East End and went visiting families to see if something could be done about the children's illnesses or truanting, escorting them to appointments with opticians or dentists. One found five or six in a bed, hardly ever a comfortable chair, not even bare essentials. Yet poor people then had no hope of a better life unless, through education or luck, somebody might rise out of his or her class. Especially in Jewish families, children were encouraged to study and if a child was bright he or she could get ahead. I remember one woman who had absolutely nothing – I can remember her dusting the kitchen chair for me to sit down – but she had a son at Cambridge and she had pawned things to buy him a dress suit he needed for some grand occasion.

The garment makers' union grew stronger. There were outcries against sweat-shop conditions and Factory Acts were passed but similar conditions arise again and again with the successive waves of immigrants. As with the Jews in the Twenties and Thirties, now in the East End Asians are badly exploited, living in overcrowded homes, hated and persecuted just as Jews were before them.

At the political meetings, I longed to join in. I wanted desperately to ask a question but I didn't dare. I would go hot and cold and blush scarlet at the very thought of it. My heart would thump and I'd go away and on the way home I was angry at my stupidity. Nobody ever spoke to me because I never spoke to anybody. I'd creep in by myself because there was nobody among our family or my friends who wanted to go. They all thought I was a little bit odd. My father encouraged me to think and do things but my mother was totally negative.

When I started going to the meetings I knew I was bourgeois. Although I was working hard for my father, he didn't make any concessions. I was like one of the workers, the lowest form of life in the workroom. Then I graduated to the showroom and I did a lot of sketching but when I went home I had every possible comfort. We had a house to ourselves and a car and a chauffeur and I had beautiful clothes, parties and plenty to eat. I didn't identify with the working class myself but I felt that society was so unjust and unfair. I suppose I always felt this guilt that I had so much when other people had so little. But I was never able to give it all away and go and live with the workers in the East End. I didn't identify with them to that extent. Nevertheless, I always felt I had to work to change society. While enjoying the benefits of being in another section, I thought society could be changed through politics.

Settling down to married life and not being all that keen on just doing housework, I continued working for my father until I had a child. Hampstead Garden Suburb had been planned as a mixed community, but after the war the tiny workers' cottages were gentrified and taken over by middle class people, so the 'mixed' society became suburban. I became Secretary of the local Labour Party ward. One of my neighbours was the Chairman – he's now a judge, Sir Neil Lawson – and he taught me a lot about politics and still does. At the same time, at the Workers' Education Association we met and read books and discussed them. Everyone had to take a turn at introducing the Book of the Month. Then the Left Book Club was started by publisher Victor Gollancz and every month a book came out in orange covers about some aspect of Socialism. So that was liberating for me, having to read a book a month – very good books indeed, about politics, about trade unionism, about China, about the Russian Revolution, about capitalism. I remember particularly a wonderful book, *The Town that was Murdered* by Ellen Wilkinson, which was about Newcastle. When my turn came to introduce the book I was absolutely terrified but that was the beginning of learning to speak in public, although these were just small meetings in people's houses. I got more and more involved and more and more knowledgeable about the whole movement and about politics.

In those days I had a lot of sympathy with the Russian Revolution but I could never quite go along with Communism, because of a horror of violence, which leads only to more violent reactions – although there was a time when I supported the National Front in France, when Labour and Communists would work closely together. I can remember some of us were warned that the Labour Party might expel one for involvement in organisations too closely allied to Communism. We've always had a broad spectrum of opinion in the Labour Party, almost-communist revolutionaries through to evolutionary democrats who are rather afraid of real change. The basis of Socialism was for the workers to own the means of production, distribution and exchange. There was the famous Clause 4 which seems to have had little importance in the Labour Party until 1994 when it became the subject of furious debate. I still think that we want some new form of ownership of land and property and capital. Money makes money. Usury is more profitable than the production of goods and services. Communist dictatorship has failed more miserably than Capitalism. Now our whole world is in danger, both ecologically and economically. New problems cry out for new solutions; old ideas give no guidance. Where are the new prophets to lead us from chaos?

Other great changes came with the rise of Fascism and Hitler. I don't think young people today can understand the extent of our painfully altered attitudes during the decade of the Thirties. We thought human beings were rational. We hadn't studied Freud much at that stage. Although I had read him I didn't really understand his ideas. The great task was to try to reconcile Freud and Marx.

This has been a major conflict all my life because one can choose whatever motives seem to fit (love or guilt, one's natural human feelings or ratiocination), yet most people believe, as I do, that one's life or some part of one's life should be used to make the world a better place. Do you do this by changing the environment through politics or do you change people from within in the psychological sense? Do people create their environment or are people shaped by their environment? I've never solved this problem, although I have worked in both the political and psychological arenas.

When I was interested in the Child Guidance movement we organised a debate between Barbara Low, one of the very first women psychoanalysts, and John Strachey who was a Marxist Socialist. The question was whether psychological or political factors are the causes of world unrest. Barbara Low won the debate for psychology.

Women had had the vote since 1918 but it seemed to me that we contemporary women were not worthy of the suffragettes who worked and sacrificed so much for us. We just weren't taking advantage. There have always been so few women in Parliament or in local government. I thought this was dreadful. I didn't really have any political ambitions for myself at the time. I just wanted to play my part in the Party but I always hoped that women would have full equality of opportunity and wages and so on. I felt that very strongly but it somehow didn't happen. The Labour Party had women's sections, mainly for the women to make the tea or organise jumble sales, but gradually women changed and worked more closely and somewhat more equally with men. Later feminist influences brought back women's sections but we are still very far from equality or the means to achieve it.

Mark was a natural left-winger but he was too busy working to get very involved, although he always supported me. There were two things, however, that he couldn't express – tenderness and emotions. He was never jealous of men friends. I think he might have been jealous of women with whom I could have serious conversations about psychological ideas and express deep feelings that he would not or could not share. He prided himself on being a very independent person and not possessive. If he thought I liked a man he would say, "Why don't you go off for the weekend with him? Get it out of your system." I always used to say I was envious because he'd had so much sexual experience and I hadn't, so he'd retort with the question, "What's stopping you?" That was actually very clever. It was rather like my father when he had stopped my unsuitable affair with the Major. Mark was very sure of me. There was a terrific bond between us.

Once Mark summed up our differences by saying that in a fatal accident, he would get the ambulance and do anything practical and necessary, whereas I would sit down and puzzle out how and why it happened.

* * *

Fashions about having babies change enormously. As with my clothes and my reading, I always had to keep up to date and in 1933 Twilight Sleep was recommended whereby you were totally unconscious during the birth of the baby. According to my doctor, I was fighting all night. It was a long, protracted delivery because I wasn't helping at all. I was anaesthetised and Lawrence, poor baby, arrived with his head pushed into a point. He must have suffered agonising birth trauma but we did not know about such things in those days. But there he was, a healthy boy, and I was absolutely delighted and his head quickly settled into a normal shape.

We had a maid from the beginning but I resolved to look after the baby myself. Josephine shared our pleasures and worries and I received loving letters from her until her daughter informed me of her death in 1986. She wrote regularly from Ireland, often mentioning that the happiest days of her life were the years she had spent with me and Mark and our two babies. Although she married and had four children of her own and many grandchildren, she looked back on her twelve years in London, when she was earning £1 a week, as blissful. So much for stories of the hardship and misery of servants. In earlier days and other classes, rich and poor, there was exploitation and distress, but in the years before the war girls like Jose in homes like ours were friends and helpmates.

I like physical things. I liked my pregnant body and its changes and I enjoyed breast feeding. I did it all very deliberately and self-consciously. I don't think I was naturally a very good mother because I'd never liked playing with dolls and babies – I only wanted books. I did my best, however, and tried whatever was fashionable then via the latest books. Truby King was in vogue, which was absolutely awful viewed from a modern angle. You were enjoined to feed your babies regularly. Even if they screamed their heads off you had regular play times and were told not to handle them too much. How my poor child survived and grew up, I just don't know. By the time I had Michael, my second child, everything was quite different. After Sigmund Freud and Anna Freud new methods came on the scene: self-demand feeding, a much more liberal regime and far less toilet training. Before that time, we put enormous emphasis on toilet training and we boasted to each other about how to avoid dirty nappies. This was very practical at the time because we didn't have washing machines. Indeed, I didn't even have a mangle. You put your nappies in to soak and then you washed them by hand. Detergents had not been invented so you used soap or soapflakes and you didn't put soda in the water because that was bad for the baby's bottom. The result was that you had thick scum round the basins and buckets to clean off and you would scrape the skin off your hands through several rinsing waters. Modern young people don't realise what hard work it was – all the many things that had to be done in a home with human energy alone. I don't remember rubber gloves at all. When were they invented? Life without disposable things – sanitary towels, tampons, tissues, plastics, detergents – is hard to visualise when now we take for granted washing machines, refrigerators, frozen foods and hundreds of our newer inventions.

In those days few mothers had their babies in hospital. Rather you had them at home with a midwife. If you were poor the midwife would just call, but if you were well enough off you would have a midwife to come and stay with you. A monthly nurse, she was called, and you'd book her in advance; too bad if baby was late. These nurses were well known to the family and friends and the same nurse would come for each child and be recommended. She would stay for three weeks while the new mother would stay in bed. Relatives and friends would come, bringing flowers and presents and the midwife would take care of the baby and teach you how to follow her example. She would help you to look after your breasts if you were breast feeding or prepare food if you couldn't. She taught you how to wash nappies and baby clothes. Other mothers would come during these proceedings to help.

Men were kept totally out of the scene during the birth and after. Mark was told to play bridge or billiards with my father. At the time I experienced a vague resentment that my husband didn't come and sit with me, holding my hand while I was having new babies, but it was not done in those days. It was so much a woman's thing. Women would come and talk about it all, especially how to get your figure back. Fathers are quite different now: shared parenting is encouraged.

Having a maid meant I could leave the babies and go out whenever I wished. Once we went to a party and came home very late, quite forgetting we had a baby. As he did not wake or cry, he did not get his late night feed ever again. Although I remember Mark often kicking me in the night to say, "Your

Michael, Lawrence and me in 1937

baby's crying", generally he was in advance of his time and keen to help. My mother was horrified at the idea of a man enjoying taking the baby out and pushing the pram: "Men don't do these things." Although Mark enjoyed helping to care for his babies, he was not like my son, Michael, who was present at the birth of his babies, entering fully into the process of relaxation and preparation for the birth and sharing fully the care of the children. There have been enormous changes and these days parents can be interchangeable except for gestation, birth and breast feeding.

I had read Freud but I didn't relate it to the care of my children until after the second child. It hadn't penetrated to that extent, so I always chastise myself for what I did to my first-born by these Truby King methods. I think mine was the first generation to read books about childcare. My mother did things the way her mother taught her as women had for generations. Then suddenly there was a complete change. We had books, but I think the baby would have responded better to my grandmother's methods.

I remember my grandmother coming to see me one day. She watched me put the child to bed in a room all by himself with the windows wide open and she said, "Are you going to leave that little baby like that all night with the window open?" I said, "Of course. My book says so." I was quite sure at the time I was right, whereas I think now, looking back, that it would have been much better to do as the older generations did – take the baby to bed and cuddle and comfort.

When I was expecting my second child I thought I should learn more about child psychology so I attended some meetings. That was where I met Dorothy Archibald who was to become a close friend and one of the most powerful influences in my life. She was always a pioneer and was about to start a charitable venture – a child guidance clinic in North West London. At this time most people thought it an absurd idea as surely children did not have psychological problems. Ours was only the third such clinic to be set up in England.

Dorothy had enormous drive and energy and inestimable charm. She obtained premises, financial support and professional advice. As a member of her committee, I was an enthusiastic worker. At that time each child was seen by a psychiatrist and psychologist while a social worker would visit the child's home and school. Psychiatric workers were trained in the USA and only later in Britain, so volunteers like myself acted as social workers under the guidance and supervision of the professionals. Once we were able to employ a trained psychiatric social worker, volunteers turned their energies to fundraising. A study group was set up where I learnt a great deal from psychoanalysts such as Barbara Low. She had been a teacher and became a close friend of the Freud family. I got to know her well. She had three sisters. One was Florence, who ran a paper called *Careers For Women.* I enjoyed listening to her arguments for and against psychoanalysis. Careers for women was always the only answer for

Florence. Neither Barbara nor Florence married. Ivy met and married Litvinov, the Russian Ambassador, and spent most of her life as a Communist in Russia, while the youngest sister married Dr David Eder, a well known psychoanalyst. Her main interest was Israel and Zionism. All four were role models for me, promoting different interests that became important in my life. The story of these four sisters would make a fascinating book.

Another teacher was Dr Sybille Yates, the only psychoanalyst I have ever known who spent her whole working life in a mental hospital and did not see private patients. She pioneered community care run from the hospital and involving local people in daytime activities. Through these teachers and others, a small group learnt to give talks in order to raise money and spread awareness of the need for therapy for children. In this activity I learnt to overcome my shyness and to speak in public.

* * *

Before I married I said to Mark, "I think marriage is an awful trap. I'm never going to be like my mother and I want my freedom," and I quoted Bertrand Russell and H G Wells. He didn't think I really meant it but he said, "Yes, dear". So in 1932, after only 18 months of marriage, I went to Russia. The family circle was absolutely horrified.

Mark and his friend John Farley married about the same time (1930) and when their two new wives met we became friends instantaneously. We had a great deal in common, sharing many interests and the same leftish views. Ina was a teacher but had had to give up her job on marriage because unemployment caused many jobs to be reserved exclusively for men or single women. The desire for a family became too strong and in spite of regrets over a career, Ina became pregnant. Alas, her first baby was stillborn.

I had seen a trip advertised: three weeks on a Russian boat from London Bridge for £25. I told my husband I'd like to go and he told John. John said to Ina, "What do you think? Rose is thinking of going to Russia!" So she rang me and said, "Do you mean it?" I said, "Well, if you'll come, I'll go", and she said, "If you'll go, I'll go. It might cheer me up!" So off we went.

It was fantastic. It was so idealistic in those days. We didn't know about

Stalin's tyranny until 1935. We went on the same boat as Beatrice and Sidney Webb, my heroes of the early Fabian days, and we would sit at the same table for meals and chat with them. They were considered very bourgeois and not socialist enough by some of the communists who were on the boat. So there was plenty of argument and discussion.

I admired the Webbs very much. They were old at the time and I would defend them for being fooled. After all, there were very many good things going on in Russia and the bad things were kept hidden and didn't emerge till later. You saw people set free who had previously been exploited, persecuted and miserable. There were serfs in Russia until the 1860s. Most peasants were still illiterate but were now being taught to read and write. There were canteens, schools, hospitals and creches and the idea of liberating women was very much alive – they had nursery schools attached to every place of work. Any woman who wanted to work could bring her baby. What we didn't realise till later was that the economy was being supported by the grandmothers who queued up for food and looked after the home while the younger women worked. But there were wonderful clubs for

George Bernard Shaw on the quayside to see his co-founders of the Fabian Society....

....Beatrice and Sydney Webb, leaving by ship on a fact-finding visit to the Soviet Union

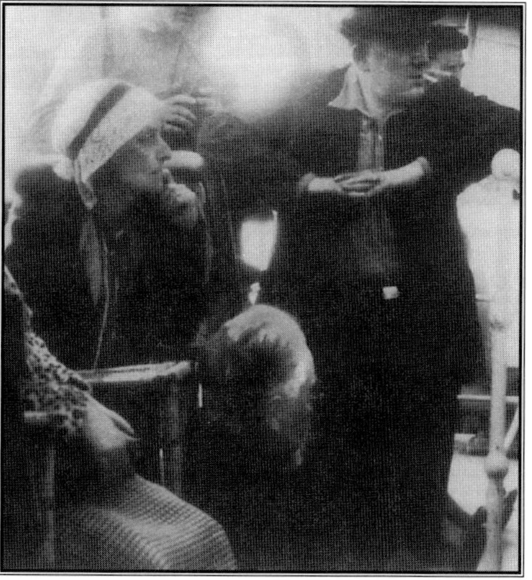

the workers and there were children's clubs and all sorts of leisure opportunities.

We did see a lot of people queueing up for food, however, and obviously there were shortages and rationing, but this seemed to be only a fair way to do things. We experienced it ourselves later during the war, but we'd never seen people queueing for food before that. There were also people obviously dispossessed; people on railway stations with their bundles. We were told they were dispossessed peasants who were coming into the towns to find work and somewhere to live. Living conditions were terrible and there was frightful overcrowding. They took us to prisons where they had very enlightened psychological methods which they changed later under Stalin. Obviously we did not see political prisoners! There was no hierarchy, there were no uniforms, but this too has all changed since. Even the crew on the boat didn't wear uniforms but rather casual clothes. Everybody mixed with everybody else. Powerful hierarchies took over but those were the heady days of the first Five Year Plan.

It was absolutely fascinating to visit Russia in 1932 because there was still this feeling of great hope for the future, a feeling of justice and equality. For example, I offered a very nice guide a pair of silk stockings. She was offended, saying, "Oh no. Only if all the women of Russia could wear silk stockings, would I wear them!" How the pendulum has swung since then!

* * *

I have friends, still alive, a little older than myself, who were involved in the Suffragette movement. Now it is accepted that women have the vote and can be active in politics, although it is sad to think how few women are in power. My role model was never my mother. I've always found other role models, more political or intellectual. Just to be the woman at home and to make a career out of being a wife and mother can never be enough. Unlike mothers of yore who died young after unceasing child care, it's now a very small part of a long life. You moan and groan and you think you will never be finished looking after the family and the home. As one woman put it, "My life is going down the kitchen sink." Many mothers talk only to toddlers and babies and suffer intellectual starvation. Yet in old age and looking back, child rearing seems only a short period and life contains many more aspects.

My early role models were personal friends like Dorothy Archibald, people who were active in the political line and in psychology. I've always realised that if you want to get anywhere as a woman you have to be a lot better than the men. And I've even been in the position where I've been the only woman, working with men, so I have thought a great deal about gender. I've never been the kind of woman who uses woman's wiles. I remember a man once saying to me as a great compliment, "Being with you is like being with another man." I liked that. I suppose because I had a good marriage I was not sexually interested in other men. Also I've had very deep friendships with women, quite different from friendships with men, where you let your back hair down and talk the same language and get very close. I have had great support from women friends.

I have had few friends who were lesbians. I remember the first time I ever heard about it was reading Radclyffe Hall's *The Well of Loneliness.* I told my mother about the book and she simply didn't believe it. There was total ignorance about lesbianism in the circles that I knew. But of course when one started to read some of the French books of the day, like Marcel Proust, a great revelation burst upon me. I did meet some girls later who had received amorous advances from other girls, especially in finishing schools abroad.

I've thought about lesbianism but I've only imagined it in relation to myself. If I have sexual needs it is for a man but I suppose if I'd had other experiences maybe I could have been a lesbian. I believe anybody can be anything. It depends upon your conditioning or upbringing, your religious convictions or whatever. So I have every sympathy with lesbians but I haven't much sympathy with women who hate men. For young women there has been a long period of feminism. I have not been very active in feminist movements, although I've always been a kind of feminist because I didn't want to be like my mother. I wanted to do other things, and I have. I think I could have achieved more if I hadn't had a husband and children. It is very difficult to get right to the top while being a wife and mother. My children's generation are different. One of my daughters-in-law, for example, combined bringing up children with working for a degree. I'm full of admiration for modern young women who cope. They have very little support, whereas I did only voluntary work and had a full-time maid. When I had my second baby I had a nanny as well, together with two people living in to help me. Of course, when the war came all that disappeared. Unused to doing all my own housework, I would sometimes cry with frustration because I was so inept.

I encountered what is often called the Second Feminist Wave, the feminism of the late Sixties, just through books. I read Betty Friedan, Kate Millett and, of course, Simone de Beauvoir and Doris Lessing. There are so many writers who have influenced me a great deal, too numerous to mention. The women I met in politics weren't the feminist ones; they were much older. It's the young ones who are into consciousness-raising and so on. My group were too busy building the welfare state.

The contacts I've had with socialist feminists are with women who are much younger. I prefer working with men and women. In the Labour Party we used to have women's sections. Then they became less popular but more recently they have revived. The first meeting of the new women's section of the local Labour Party took place in my house. It must have been in the 1960s or early 1970s. Young women, who were new members of the Party, wanted to form a women's group. Edith Summerskill and Millie Miller attended – both my mentors.

* * *

It's hard to describe the impact of Hitler and the shock of fascism to one's whole philosophy of life. That man was not rational and I had always thought the Germans were well-educated, intellectual people. I often met young Germans who had had a much better education in their schools than we had. Suddenly there they were – mad people. Being Jewish, this was a terrific shock to me: the idea that people that you admired as intelligent were a long way from being rational beings. It was a terrible setback. Of course, during the whole of the war I was working in the context of Labour Party and Anglo-Soviet friendship. There were lots of meetings to try to understand the Russian Revolution and their constitution and aims. They were our allies and they suffered even more than we did, much more. Sixty million Russians were killed and whole areas devastated. At our meetings we hopefully discussed our victory over fascism and how the United Nations would usher in a new era of peace and friendship and social justice.

The War Years

We are born in relationship, nurtured in relationship and educated in relationship. We represent every biological and social relationship of our forbears, as we interact and exist in a consensual domain called society.
Mary Hughes – Lecture to the Progressive League, "Being Here, Relating, AIDS and the Game Boy" 26.2.93

It is not easy to recapture the mood and the mode of the war years. The sound of sirens still churns my stomach. The memory of rationing and coupons, echoing the shortages of the First World War, gives me an outrageous sense of guilt over wasted food to this day. Evacuation, fire drills, stirrup pumps, gas masks, air raid shelters, digging for victory, sharing homes, the cloud of fear and the waiting, waiting, waiting for letters, for news. The terror and the destruction, abroad and at home and the horrors of capture and death of loved ones. My brother and brother-in-law in the Royal Air Force, Mark's brother in the Army, Mark fire-watching in London.

The main preoccupation of all parents was the safety of our children. Just before war was declared Michael, my three year old, caught scarlet fever. Notifiable diseases were taken very seriously in those days and I was offered a choice: to send him to a 'Fever Hospital' or to send Lawrence, my six year old, away from infection. I decided to nurse Michael at home and send Lawrence to my mother. We had to hang a disinfectant-soaked sheet over the bedroom door and keep him isolated for several weeks. Everything in his room had to be sent away to be fumigated. Such extraordinary precautions, thank heavens, are now a thing of the past. By the time the risk of infection had passed war had been declared and we had decided to leave London.

Poor Lawrence was sent to stay with my parents but they had made previous plans to go away, so he had to go to a 'children's hotel'. By the time

Michael's quarantine period was over we were in Brighton where friends had offered us a refuge from the expected bombing raids. Curiously, I was repeating my mother's flight to Brighton with us, her children, during World War I. I felt sad and guilty when at last I could fetch my son. I realised that he had suddenly lost his home, his toys, his school friends and all familiar things and surroundings, never to see them again. How he has survived without major neuroses is a mystery to me.

From Brighton, which was not considered safe, we moved to a rented house in Cranleigh, Surrey, because the school Lawrence had attended in Hampstead had moved there and become a boarding school. I was to have the extra children in a second house if there were too many for the original house, but in the event there were no extra children. We stayed in Cranleigh for about a year and, as the Battle of Britain hotted up, we saw planes falling in spirals of smoke and a stick of bombs descended nearby. I often think of how different subsequent history might have been if these gallant young air crews had lived to provide the leaders and thinkers this second half of the century has lacked.

Philip in his RAF uniform

We really expected Hitler to invade England, probably somewhere along the South or East coast. As Jews, we anticipated the fate of French and Dutch Jews who had joined their German co-religionists in the concentration camps. Mark tried to persuade me to take the boys to America but I refused until it was too late for ships to travel. Although bombing was heavy in London and his Holborn office building was hit three times, he would never talk about his experience but constantly discussed safer homes for me and the children.

In Cranleigh neighbours were kind and helpful and a childless couple offered, in the event of a Nazi invasion, to take my children and pretend they were their own. As my boys were fair-skinned with red hair they could pass for Aryans. It was moving to receive such generosity and heart-warming to realise that our new friends would take such risks for strangers. Surely it must be true, and my experience confirms, that humans are more often loving and co-operative than cruel, greedy and murderous. In wartime one sees so clearly the conflicts within individuals as well as in large groups and nations.

Mark insisted that we move somewhere safer so we left Cranleigh and our kind neighbours and went to a farm in Trefnant, North Wales. Here the children caught chicken pox. The rooms were unheated and I spent the worst Xmas and New Year of my life. I used to cry trying to light a fire when paper and wood were in short supply. Sometimes a glass of water at the children's bedside was frozen solid in the morning. My sister came for Xmas. Her husband was in the Air Force and we spent a miserable time together trying to amuse the boys and assuage the irritation of their spots. The family with whom we were lodging would not come near us: they thought that the cows might catch chicken pox.

Then we moved to a country house in Shropshire where a widow took in paying guests. Other boarders included an elderly lady and her wretched companion whom she called 'Fool' and bullied mercilessly. Michael constantly made embarrassing remarks such as, "Why have you got hair on your face?"

The food was ghastly and, although rationed, it need not have been so sparse. Once they obtained a pig which had been secretly slaughtered but we never had a good roast joint. For days we seemed to exist on pigs ears, trotters, innards and sundry gristly bits and pieces.

I grew to hate the country. There was no piped water and the hand pump was difficult to manipulate. The boys fell into cowpats and the shortage of water – let alone hot water – was not my idea of fun! I had to leave this dreadful place.

At one stage of our wanderings in search of safety, I sent the boys to A S Neill's Summerhill, a progressive school where children were free to choose to attend lessons or not. Neill had moved his school from Leiston in Suffolk to a large house in Blaenau Festiniog. This corner of North Wales seemed most unlikely to be bombed or invaded. Ina and I had long admired Neill and read his books but we did not leave our children there for long. The little ones were well cared for by a delightful young woman (a relative of Neill's) and her Indian husband but the seven year olds were quite miserable. Mrs Neill was seriously ill and died that year. Neill hated the Welsh mountains and had too generously accepted too many children and many new staff unused to the ways of Summerhill. To my mind the children were at the mercy of each other and the lack of any kind of framework was too 'progressive', even for us.

Meanwhile Mark was afraid for the safety of his clients' documents and had been offered some space in a factory in Leicester. I took a suitcase and went to a hotel there, intending to look for another home where perhaps Mark could commute. During the whole of the war there were only two raids on Leicester on consecutive nights and I had to be there for both! On my first night, alone in a strange town, I saw an advertisement for a political meeting and went along. As I walked back to the hotel the sirens went off and people ran to shelters. I loathe shelters and preferred to walk on to the hotel. It was a fire-bomb raid and I heard the ghastly whine followed by the explosions. As I neared the hotel I saw it was on fire! I rushed in and up to my room and all I can remember of the things I hastily snatched is a pair of good leather shoes. I was not allowed to go back into the hotel so my carefully selected little treasures went up in smoke: some favourite books and gramophone records and the baby-record books we used to keep to remind us of a child's first step, first word, birthday parties and snapshots in black and white.

Excellent arrangements were made for homeless victims of air raids. We were found billets, given coupons for the replacement of lost clothes and I stayed with a Mrs Barnett who could not have been kinder or more helpful. She had already lost a son in the war and a little girl had died in childhood. Her only remaining son married a clever and beautiful woman who became a TV celebrity and died tragically.

I was a member of the Women's Voluntary Society (WVS) and found plenty to do in Leicestershire: transporting people and supplies from bombed cities to billets in the countryside and often driving in the blackout without lights and finding my way at night.

Longing to unite the family and never wanting boarding school for my children, I was delighted to read an advertisement in the *New Statesman*: "Rooms available for family. Any race or religion. Near progressive school. Possible access London." This was Eve Shannon's protest against neighbours who advertised "No Jews or foreigners". It seemed made for us so I telephoned Mark and told him to get in touch. When he phoned me back he said he had only two objections. One, it was in Letchworth where there were factories and he would have preferred a more rural environment. Two, if we went to live there we would never get a home of our own. With his percipience he realised that Eve was my sort of person and that I would settle happily in her home, which resembled my own, and not bother to look further and, of course, he was right.

There was no question of renting rooms. Eve and her daughter and I and my sons lived communally, sharing chores and expenses. Mark came at weekends as the bombing of London worsened. We grew vegetables, kept chickens and ducks, took our turns at fire-watching, ferried children to and from school on the back of our bicycles and did all kinds of war work.

I drove a rickety van fitted with two primus stoves and kettles wired on for safety! We took NAAFI rations to lonely men and women on searchlight and anti-aircraft stations in the country and a cheer would echo as we drove up, ready to make fresh tea and coffee and deliver such shopping as they had commissioned. We never failed, whatever the weather, using chains on the tyres in snow and ice. My grandchildren when small used to enjoy wearing "Granny's Defence Medal" (my award for war service).

As the raids became more frequent and more frightening, Eve opened her heart and her home to other people fleeing London and we had makeshift beds on the sitting-room floor and our experiment in communal living expanded.

Eve's compassion was boundless; our friendship lasted until her death. After the war she devoted herself to the care of the mentally ill, ex-prisoners, the homeless. She completely ignored her age and forgot to claim her pension or retire. A typical event in Eve's later life was when the chairman of a voluntary home for mental patients ordered her to hide the artificial legs of a black patient to punish him for being aggressive. As warden of the home Eve refused because she understood the man and had gained his confidence. She knew how to handle his aggression and calm him down. To mistrust him and remove his legs would only produce anger and resentment and destroy the relationship which kept him steady. She kept her ground and was instantly dismissed without notice. Echoing her mother's example, her daughter Moira, now a professor of art history in the USA, continues to work for women's rights and for the expanded recognition and support of women and people of colour as artists.

Community living did not suit Mark, who longed for one family in one home, so eventually we bought a house in Letchworth. As our London house had been badly damaged in air raids, we stayed there until 1951. Mark gradually gave up fire-watching and commuted daily from Letchworth to London. All his spare time at weekends and evenings was spent in the Home Guard. The TV programme *Dad's Army* gives a fairly accurate picture of this outfit. Mark's German was quite good so he was in 'intelligence' out looking around the countryside for German spies and escaping aircrew or prisoners of war!

We made friends in Letchworth with fellow parents of children at St Christopher's School. There were many other evacuated Londoners and what with the WVS, the Electrical Association for Women, the Labour Party, the

Letchworth Electrical Association for Women (WVS). I'm fifth from the right, wearing the Defence Medal for War Service. In the van are the primus stoves, on which we boiled the kettles while we drove NAAFI rations in all weathers to anti-aircraft and searchlight stations

Anglo-Soviet Friendship Society, the Music Society and many other organisations, we were always busy. I spent some time helping Tom Harrison and his assistants who ran Mass Observation. Modern computer-trained people would roar with laughter if they could see how we analysed the documents we collected and how we stored them all in files in the attic of Tom's house.

In our own home we were not alone for long. Mark's brother-in-law died, so his sister and her two children joined us and, because London had become too dangerous for them, my parents came to stay for a time. How we all fitted in was a miracle. Now that I find it too much trouble to cook for myself alone, I can't imagine how I cooked every day for nine of us and managed simultaneously all the outside activities for the war effort!

Letchworth Garden City was an interesting place to live, quite apart from the relief at being away from the bombs. The town contrasted with Hampstead Garden Suburb in that it was built to include factories. Homes and factories were on tree-lined streets and the plans allowed one to walk or cycle from home to work. Letchworth was designed to help unemployed families from Northern and Midland cities settle in a new and healthier environment and obtain work in new factories. The population was very mixed; there were churches and societies of all denominations and many adult education opportunities.

There were no pubs in the town but well-worn tracks across the fields led to the pubs in the villages surrounding the town. Drinks were available, though, at the Golf Club and the Letchworth Hall Hotel. Rotary clubs flourished and the many clubs and groups ran charity dances and so forth, so there was no lack of social life. There was a clear division between the classes, however, although this was never the intention of the founders. At the top were the members of the Golf Club and the professional people who did not mix with the factory workers socially. Although to some extent the Educational Institute, the Labour Party, the Home Guard and the WVS broke down barriers during the war, in peacetime class divisions were speedily re-established.

St Christopher's was a progressive school. They advertised their method as "ordered freedom". Early classes were run on Montessori principles and Madame Montessori herself once came to lecture to parents. I remember her

Mark as a sergeant in the Letchworth Home Guard, second from the right

rather quaint English; eventually she gave up and spoke in Italian, her son translating as she proceeded. She advocated a period of work for all children before considering higher education. Work in the real world could enable wiser choices and increased benefit from degree courses. I still think this an excellent idea and young people nowadays often adopt this pattern.

St Christopher's was run by a remarkable Quaker couple, Mr and Mrs Harris, but the school itself was nondemonimational. They believed in educating the parents so we attended lectures regularly and learnt about vegetarian diet and made our own muesli and wholemeal bread for many years.

I have never regretted, nor have my sons, the choice of this school. Co-educational and run on the lines of a modified Dalton plan, it gave each child an individual assignment but no homework. The day was organised so that written work was done in school time. There was music, drama and art at all levels and the aim was a balanced, all-round development. The boys were happy there.

My mother kept all the letters my children wrote during the war.

Although they drew pictures of aeroplanes and asked about bombs and air-raids, they mostly wrote thanks for presents and money and sweets. (My parents sent their rations to the children.) The boys asked for what they wanted in detail. They seemed to accept wartime conditions as I had once done long before. My mother had also kept letters that I wrote during the 1914–18 war. One shows a map of Germany being destroyed.

* * *

Before and during the war and for decades afterwards, my life and politics were enriched by a remarkable series of friendships, many of which evolved through an equally remarkable context, that of a Co-operative Correspondence Club (CCC) which was begun in 1935.

It all began through *The Nursery World,* a magazine read by many conscientious young mothers in the Twenties and Thirties. In this periodical we read about how to care for our babies. There were advertisements to sell or buy second-hand prams, cots and clothing, and to engage a nanny or mother's help. Ours was the first generation to read books and magazines instead of simply absorbing the experience of mothers and grandmothers, and the first generation of women who had the knowledge and the will to practise birth control.

Ubique (everyone had a pen name) was a reader of *The Nursery World.* She thought it might be interesting to get to know some of the women whose letters appealed to her when she read the pages of correspondence entitled 'Over the Tea Cups'. Ubique herself was a lively and interesting writer, a supporter of Irish Independence and a Roman Catholic of firm views. I remember many an argument about sex and in our magazine there were great discussions about coitus reservatus and coitus interruptus and other methods of birth control as and when they were invented.

Ubique's idea of the Co-operative Correspondence Club caught on: she kept the magazine going for all the years before the war and during the first years of the war. Wartime brought censorship of letters and packages and the blue pencil and blacked-out passages were irritating to say the least. Finally we decided it was impossible to have the magazine edited and sent out from Eire. It was then that Ad Astra took over the editorship until she was too disabled to continue.

Ad Astra was, in reality, my friend Ina Farley with whom I had travelled to Russia in 1932. It was Ad Astra/Ina who recruited me to the CCC although I had never been a correspondent to *The Nursery World.* It was the goal of the group to gather women of varied backgrounds – different classes and ethnicities – yet some of the earliest copies of the CCC magazine had contained quite anti-Semitic articles which had worried Ad Astra. This was the time of Hitler's rise to power. As a Jew I accepted this challenge of confronting articles which dealt with such themes as "Jews are an irritant in the body-politic" and "Jews succeed in business through unfair competition" and so forth. For my pseudonym I chose Elektra – for obvious reasons!

For some time I found my CCC membership a source of pain and unhappiness but there was much support in the early pages of our magazine, especially from Ad Astra and several others and gradually we all came to an understanding. Quite a few members befriended Jewish refugees and, although I am sure prejudice never completely dies, it was kept under control and reason prevailed, at least in our writings. Ad Astra's discretion and compassion always kept the arguments from getting out of hand or being hurtful or insulting, although nothing was ever withheld or censored or abbreviated.

Under Ubique's original leadership the CCC was organised as follows. Each of the twenty four members was required to write at least once a month on any subject and send the notes in handwriting or typed (but few owned a typewriter) to Ubique who would punch holes and sew them together in a linen cover, often hand-embroidered. This would be sent with a note from member to member. Each mother would have to read and send it on within twenty four hours to the next name on a rota list. Remarks were written in the margins of the articles agreeing or disputing with statements and these opinions led to lively and sometimes acrimonious debate and discussion.

We wrote about our families: the best ways of feeding children, washing nappies, coping with temper tantrums or refusals to eat, menstruation and its problems, keeping husbands happy and well fed, coping with the conflicting demands of husbands and children, sex and birth control and so on.

In 1939 the war introduced a different flavour to the magazine. Rationing led to the exchange of economical recipes. Many members moved from town to the country with their children. Some children were sent to boarding school or to stay with friends or relatives. None of these children had to take a chance of being billetted with strangers, like so many children from the towns. In old or new homes CCC members took on new roles as war workers, often in the ARP carrying out air raid precaution duties such as fitting gas masks, practising fire fighting or gas attack defences. Some joined the WVS and earned the Defence medal for various regular and sustained war work. Our writings reflect the heartache of separation from husbands in the forces, or prisoners of war, or fire-watching and fire-fighting and clearing up after bombings of office and business premises or homes in towns while families were away.

What a boon was our regular magazine in those bleak and lonely years. We became closer than ever and visited each other whenever we were billetted near or could travel. We took the greatest interest in each other's children who often became friends. In emergencies we often sent our children to other members living in safer places.

It is difficult to evaluate the changes after the war. It was a long time before rationing ended. 'Make-do and mend' was still a way of life and 'digging for victory' continued as producing fruit and vegetables or keeping chickens to supplement the diet. Looking back, these women were proud of the health of their children, considerably better than that of children in more recent times of unlimited choice and quantity of food. The return of husbands, change of address to former homes or to new homes, the re-adjustment of living in families again and the new post-war babies to be welcomed were all written about. For most there were never again to be maids or nannies and young grannies found themselves a major support of grandchildren.

It is fascinating, too, to read about the new interests and occupations once war work and child-minding were no longer necessary. Some women had jobs. It was important to add to the family income and almost all developed a latent or new-found talent. There were many writers; some succeeded in having short stories or articles published in local papers or magazines. We find examples of painting, marquetry, sculpture, flower-arranging, embroidery, patchwork and upholstery. Many were adept at decorating the home, painting walls, paper-hanging and so on. Gardening occupied many of the members; bird-watching was taken seriously; chess and crossword puzzles absorbed the more intellectual, even when they became bed-ridden.

Women's Institutes, church groups, peace organisations and political activities attracted some members and voluntary work such as Marriage Guidance and the Samaritans absorbed the spare time of several. All seemed to read a great deal and books were recommended and discussed. A number took a great interest in poetry and often quoted from favourite authors in the magazine. Some wrote their own poems and at one time members put stars in the margin to acclaim special literary merit or outstanding interest.

During and after World War II, our group of twenty four women became more intimate and frank and some who lived near enough formed close and regular associations. Ongoing issues of religion and politics absorbed us as our interests widened as children grew up and produced new families. We took for granted that if anywhere near we could visit and stay. There were regular meetings in London and it was a fascinating experience to meet in the flesh those we knew so well on paper.

How did we women who, on the surface, seemed to have so little in common, form such a close and affectionate network of genuine friendship, caring and sympathising and giving support? We were not selected, simply invited on the strength of a letter to a journal or introduced by an existing member as a possible contributor of interesting articles. None of us would have met in our own networks of close friends and acquaintances. Our differences drew us together. We all seemed to be open-minded and genuinely interested in learning how others coped with their lives. We all had to do housework, bring up children, make our marriages and family relationships work. We lived in different kinds of homes, in town, country or suburb. There were endless ways of living so a lively curiosity and a non-judgmental attitude were essential.

The amazing thing is how our friendship and loving support has sustained us in spite of the vast differences in upbringing, income, religion, politics, our different ways of bringing up children and contrasting ideas about education. There has been an increase in tolerance, love and understanding and an underlying quest for knowledge and truth, with a strong need to establish our own individual philosophy of life and a longing to find some pattern or meaning in our lives.

I suppose one answer to why we stayed together is that Rudyard Kipling was right that "the Colonel's lady and Judy O'Grady are sisters under the skin"! Our first priority was home, husband and children and human loving relationships imperative to be worked for. As in all families, rows and arguments were inevitable, but there seem to have been genuine efforts to understand different points of view and many reconciliations.

The spontaneity and the frankness of the writing, which shows women writing in the heat of a new experience, whether pleasure or pain, ecstasy or sorrow, led to a sympathetic response and honesty begat honesty, so that we felt that we knew each other better than even close friends or relatives.

Believe it or not our magazine – which we had begun in 1935 – lasted for over fifty four years. The magazine finally ended at Christmas 1989, as this was the last number to be edited by Ad Astra. For years I would visit her two or three times a year and we were in touch by telephone two or three times a week. What a boon the 'phone is to old people and as long as one can hear, the contact with old friends is an important source of support and pleasure.

We six who are left keep in touch by sending a notebook on a rota and, as we receive it, we write a few pages to keep us all in touch with our doings and news of families.

* * *

After the war ended there were innumerable changes in our lives, but for me the most traumatic was the death of my beloved father.

In 1947 we came home from our holiday in France to find Daddy ill in bed. He had had a chill for about four days and looked ghastly. For a whole month we watched him getting weaker and weaker, feeling wretched, helpless and impotent. At least we had the consolation of knowing that he felt no pain or distress and we were all with him at the end, though I do not think he knew any of us. There was a day between life and death when it was hard to tell, but his eyes were open and very blue.

He was an elderly man and had lived a full and complete life. At seventy two I suppose it is no tragedy to die peacefully, but somehow it is very hard to accept it in that light. Often as I watched him I could not realise that he was really seventy two. I have always thought of him as so young – younger in thought and mind than many of my contemporaries – and between us there was that very special kind of understanding that one sometimes finds between father and daughter when the temperaments are similar. Even the nurses noticed that he was somehow different with me. Now he is gone and there will never ever again be that particular kind of contact with anyone.

We shared so much. We worked together in business for many years and we shared many pleasures: books, music, good food, delight in line and colour and artistic expression. And he was so completely understanding. His great virtue was his ability to leave me alone to follow my own lines of development. In my early twenties I had made spasmodic attempts to break away from his plan to have me in business with him, yet this tie – though gentle and silken – was too strong for me to break despite my vague aspirations towards a more artistic and intellectual job.

My father had many faults yet when one considers his life it is amazing that his faults were so few and so mild and that he was universally adored. Of the hundreds who came to his funeral, very few were not sincere mourners. All of them missed him, though he often shocked and irritated his conventional friends with his outspoken and progressive opinions. All the young relatives and friends would talk to him as an equal and he loved these lively conversations.

In imagination I often live his youthful life over again. A thin, ragged child with pale face, ginger hair and blue eyes, sent off at the age of twelve as apprentice to a bookbinder. Sleeping on straw under the work-benches, he was fed like an animal with any old scraps. Beaten and bullied, yet delighting in the skilful and creative work of binding books in leather and decorating them with gold and tooling and marbled end papers.

Imagine the burning, intense desire to get away from the misery and oppression of life in Russian Poland where to be a Jew was to be a pariah, confined to ghetto quarters and excluded from schools and professions, the broad streets of the cities and the good life on the land. His one ambition was to live in a land of freedom and tolerance and to help his parents and his eight brothers and sisters to do the same.

His miserable childhood of poverty and hard work undermined his health and he suffered serious illness and an operation in his thirties. Yet he defied the doctors and lived to be seventy two, only retiring twelve years before his death. He never took a holiday and the pace at which he worked often exhausted me. All his gifts and energies were poured into business.

He was often seriously ill but somehow never missed an appointment: his vitality and will-power drove him on even if in pain. Mother had to put up with the reaction and many the sleepless night she had when he gave way to pain and distress. His retirement was spoilt by the war and much pain over prostate trouble which failed to yield to treatments of various sorts.

He and Mummy loved London and hated being away. A land mine that cracked their air raid shelter drove them from their home until his pain brought him back to London for the operations. He always appreciated so much the Masonic Hospital – he was a keen mason – and all that the nurses and doctors did for him. My parents stayed in London all the rest of the war, except for a few weeks with me in Letchworth during the buzz-bomb period. They preferred London with its dangers and alarms to Letchworth dullness. And they enjoyed their own home and friends and a game of bridge, sleeping in their own bed and taking a chance in the London way.

His operation in 1947 had been successful. The horrible and humiliating pains and difficulties were over and he seemed so well. It was a shock, therefore, to find him suddenly so ill. At first they diagnosed a streptoccal infection, then pneumonia, then infective endocarditis for which he had injections of the newly-discovered penicillin together with digitalis and coramine. But, though they kept the temperature down, his heart and pulse and respiration got weaker and weaker and he could not stand the strain. Often he could hardly whisper a word but it was usually a joke or ironic comment. We had day and night nurses who adored him. I was there during the week to help them with lifting and washing and giving oxygen. The rigors were terrible to watch.

He died beautifully in a coma, at peace in his own home. As he lay dying I came into his room. He stretched out his arms and cried, "Darling" and I rushed into his embrace. This has been forever after the most poignantly remembered moment of my life. Although in my forties, married and a mother, this revelation of the long-denied fulfilment of my deepest infantile needs confirmed all I had learnt about myself and others. The need for loving arms and the confirmation of affection never leaves us. We all need to love and be loved and to feel loved, and I was no exception. The oldest child often grows up too soon and presents a confident independent personality but the rock upon which others rely for stability is balanced precariously upon the shifting sands of unmet needs. In me the infantile desire to be cuddled and comforted has been deeply denied and a defensive armour makes it impossible for me or other seemingly strong characters to demand or accept the affection we crave. Somehow helping the nurse to lay my father out and perform those last ever personal rites was a consummation.

After the funeral I spent the night comforting my mother, wishing my father's lean, firm body was in my arms instead of my mother's hated smooth, plump softness. It was only many years later when Mother was dying of cancer that I could hold her emaciated body with love and compassion.

Father had a full and interesting life and it is not given to many to realise their ambitions. He gave happiness, hope, employment and charity to so many and never had to ask anything for himself. He was blessed with unusual courage and humour and was completely without affectation or humbug. His code was rigidly honest and just. Although he was often cynical and even bitter, he played the game according to all the rules, yet he despised the capitalist system and hoped for greater justice for the underdog. He was never ashamed of his past and did not forget that a miserable childhood like his still exists for millions. He understood how changing conditions made it impossible to follow his example. He was never smug or proud or self-righteous. He understood so well the limitations of circumstance and opportunity and historical development. His life is done and we should not grieve but I miss him still, nearly fifty years later.

The Postwar Years

And when I came upon Highgate Hill
And had a view of London
My heart was all light and joy.
Boswell

The war had affected me greatly and I was a different person at the end of it. I was in my forties, a dangerous age for women. The war was over and I was going back to London's suburbia. What was I going to do? My children were my main preoccupation but they were growing up. I loved my husband and that mysterious chemical attraction between us never weakened. Yet, though we had much in common, he could only share my increasing preoccupation with psychological matters on a practical level. He was impatient with introspective discussions.

In 1951 we moved back to London and my life began to change dramatically with my work in marriage guidance, the London County Council (later to become the Greater London Council), my association with the mental hospitals, community care and my new role as a writer-lecturer on 'education for personal relationships'. Most importantly, a live-in housekeeper made it possible for me to manage this multi-faceted career outside my home.

The year 1951 was thus a great turning point for me. My father's death just after the end of the war and then our move back to London from Letchworth had brought immense changes. There was a feeling of optimism around. The Festival of Britain brought the South Bank to life. Exhibitions convinced us that "Britain could make it". Scientific discoveries and new manufacturing techniques promised improvements in standards of living. The Festival Hall was a revelation of new building and has amply fulfilled expectations of fine music in appropriate environments. Meanwhile there was dancing round the bandstand and a note of expansion and gaiety after austerity.

For some time when we wanted to stay in London we had used a couple of rooms on the top floor of Mark's office building. Bomb damage had caused a move from Holborn to temporary premises in Regent Street and then to Maddox Street, where the practice owned the whole building, letting two floors to other firms. We shared the top floor with a couple who acted as caretakers. They owned a fierce parrot with whom I never made friends.

When Lawrence left school to study at the London School of Economics he joined us but there was little space and we longed for a real home. Then friends found a house for us on Highgate West Hill (an area made famous by John Betjeman).

The house seemed to have been built in the early Thirties, of old relics, whether from an original house or a junk yard. The doors, windows and staircase were all old and a stone terrace in front ensured that the house blended with the neighbours although inside it was smaller and simpler in plan. Wartime rationing of building materials still existed so the improvements needed seemed daunting. An old lady had lived there with nine dogs and the place had an air of neglect and Dickensian gloom. The garden was crowded with fruit trees planted too close together, between which were huts and sheds full of hoarded junk, pots of paint, pieces of wood, chicken huts and old broken-framed prints of dogs and little children.

In spite of all the drawbacks, I could see possibilities. The shape of the house was pleasing and the garden could be beautiful. Eventually we bought it, though Mark was apprehensive about all the necessary alterations, and how right he was! We had walls knocked down, installed new central heating and electric wiring, painted it in light colours instead of dark brown and spent two years of hard labour in the garden clearing the junk and gradually planting cuttings from the gardens of friends. Almost all our shrubs and perennials reminded me of someone. There was a gorgeous mulberry tree and two morello cherries, on which I would pull old stockings and tights to save the fruit from the birds.

Some plants and shrubs, including a witchhazel and a white camellia, moved with me in 1983 (after Mark's death I sold the house and bought a nearby flat) and now enhance my view from the window of the flat with memories of dear friends who gave them to me. Behind the house stretched

Parliament Hill Fields, Kenwood and Hampstead Heath with its ponds; beyond were Golders Hill Park and Hill House Gardens, the beloved haunts of my whole life with Father, Mark, sons, grandsons and dear friends. We were happy to be back in London and never regretted buying the house where we spent over thirty years.

I had always believed in progressive education and my sons enjoyed happy schooldays. As small children, before the war, they had attended local nursery school. Lawrence went to Burgess Hill School in Hampstead started by Kenneth Ottoway, a delightful school where like-minded parents participated. Meanwhile, my friend Ethel Ginsberg started up a nursery school of her own and Michael attended this. She arranged a perfect environment in the basement and garden of her house in Redington Road. The latest ideas were followed: freedom of expression, creative and imaginative play with sand and water and toys from Abbatts. *Education Through Art* by Herbert Read, as well as music and movement, were inspirational. Our mutual friend, Barbara Low, had translated Anna Freud's first book *Psychoanalysis For Teachers* and this, too, led to new initiatives in early education.

While Lawrence attended University, Michael stayed at St Christopher's for a year to take O-level exams and then returned to live with us and join the sixth form in the City of London School for Boys. One day, however, he came home and announced that he had decided not to go to medical school. Mark and I were appalled. What had happened? What did he want to do? He said, "I just want to draw and paint". We could not see a future for him as an artist but he quickly produced a portfolio of drawings and took himself round to colleges of architecture. He was offered a place at the Architectural Association School of Architecture, and subsequently enjoyed a career that developed his many talents and earned an OBE before early retirement.

Lawrence's career, too, went through many changes including accountancy and car accessories before finally, as a patent agent, he was able to use a variety of skills and enjoy a satisfying professional life. He did two years of National Service in the RAF and built himself a racing car at the weekends.

With Michael's change of heart, I felt as if blinded by a great light. After a wide and comprehensive education in a fine school where art, music and drama and social relationships were as important as academic subjects, he had endured three years of aesthetic stagnation concentrating on three scientific subjects only. The school's regime was contrary to all my cherished beliefs. This confirmed my understanding of the value of progressive education. Children need the opportunities to develop all their potential, no matter what trade or profession they intend to pursue. The arts are a necessity, not just frills on basic education. Indeed almost all subjects may be studied through art.

I observe, with deep regret, that at the present time, after a period when teachers seemed to have understood and implemented the mainsprings of learning, we are moving backwards in favour of training rather than education, and narrow training for jobs that do not exist. I really thought that progressive education, pioneered in independent schools such as Summerhill, Bedales, St Christopher's, Dartington Hall, Kisquhanity and others, had influenced state education. This was certainly true of primary schools for some time but the tide has now turned, and not for the better.

Back in London I realised how much my ideas had changed. We never again gave or went to bridge parties. Nor did we join a golf club. We chose our friends because we enjoyed their conversation and their company, not for business reasons or to make up a suitable bridge table. Many shared our interests in politics and voluntary work.

Dorothy and George Archibald remained good friends, exercising a powerful influence, especially on me. She was the substitute mother and role model, and through her I was co-opted on to the Children's Committee of the Greater London Council and also onto Friern Hospital Committee.

* * *

The London County Council, which preceded the Greater London Council, was responsible, in addition to its wider duties, for Social Welfare for young and old. Soon after the end of World War II a public scandal erupted, drawing attention to children ill-treated in foster homes over which there was no legislative control. Children were found to be neglected and abused and sometimes in real danger. A children's committee was set up, followed by an

Act of Parliament, and I was privileged to be a member of the committee which set up the first Child Assessment Centre.

We had, of course, Orphanage Homes and some were models in their time. So-called 'cottages', each housing about twenty children, were grouped around a school, gardens and play areas. Perhaps between one and two hundred children were segregated and educated apart from the local community.

I remember visiting one such home with an elderly experienced LCC member. We looked around the buildings and inspected the kitchens and bedrooms. All was clean and orderly, no sign of mess or muddle or toys and dolls and teddy bears on the beds, nothing like my own children's rooms. Boys and girls were in separate 'cottages', babies and toddlers in different homes. Siblings rarely met. Most were orphans or abandoned, but parents were allowed to visit if thought suitable. I asked about the children. They were all in school and it was an unwritten law that committee members never saw the children except on special occasions such as prize-givings. Things changed rapidly after the Children's Act was passed.

This new Assessment Centre was residential. It was situated in Langley House in East India Dock Road, a beautiful old sea captain's house in the Docklands, with a mulberry tree in what had once been a garden but was now an asphalted playground. Here, with the help of a team consisting of part-time psychiatrist and psychologist, a full-time psychiatric social worker and dedicated child care staff, each child was carefully studied and their needs assessed.

Lady Dorothy Archibald, then chairperson of Friern Hospital

Langley House was a model of its kind and the first of these new children's homes. Instead of the large institutions, different kinds of children's homes were quickly acquired and many small homes were built in the new towns that sprang up after the war. We tried to arrange to have children in small groups with a house mother. Brothers and sisters were able to live together and children went to local schools like their neighbours.

We saw that too much strain was being put upon the house mother in our efforts to make homes as much like a real family as possible. We realised that, unwittingly, we had produced a situation akin to that of a single mother with a large family; the kind of stressful life that often led to children coming into care! We then built extensions to the homes so that extra staff could live in, often married couples, sometimes with children of their own. Relief staff were appointed so that house mothers could have regular time off.

Gradually, as GLC control was passed to individual local authorities, more children were fostered and there were fewer children's homes. This time foster parents were carefully chosen and supervised by social workers. The old fashioned house parents, often single women, were totally dedicated to the children, often adopting a child or two when they retired.

Most of the children came into care because of family breakdown and this was one of the factors that led to my enthusiasm for Marriage Guidance. In happy marriages, children rarely need to be taken into care.

* * *

The Marriage Guidance Movement had begun during World War II but I only joined it in 1945. I had first heard about it at a lecture in Letchworth sponsored by St Christopher's. The talk was given by Marjorie Hume and I was inspired. I became a member. I was apprehensive at first, feeling that only psychiatrists could deal with such difficult matters, but I agreed to work with young people in schools and clubs on 'preparation for marriage'. Later we called it 'education for personal relationships'. After selection and training, I became a counsellor and gradually realised that a professional qualification was not necessarily the right approach to this task.

I remember those rooms in Duke Street where, all alone, I or another of the handful of early counsellors would wait at night and deal single-handed with anyone who had made an appointment. On the ground floor was a chemist shop and the top floor was a small brothel. What could be more appropriate? How naive we were! Much later in other premises we never allowed anyone to attend alone.

How the movement has changed since 1952! There are now branches called Relate in every town, with headquarters in Rugby. Counsellors now number thousands instead of a handful and unfortunately there are waiting lists for the service. It is a great source of satisfaction to have been a member of a small band of pioneers – often ridiculed as nosey-parkers, and once described in a newspaper article as "lumpy ladies in tweeds" (although there have been men counsellors from the beginning).

In 1956 I wrote my first book in the context of my work in marriage guidance and education of young people in personal relationships. I had given many talks on the subject and one day I said to Mark: "Look, I have been keeping notes for ten years about questions that children and young people have asked. I could write books about this and then I wouldn't have to go round talking about it." Mark said, "Why don't you?" and I responded with, "I have too much respect for the craft of writing and for writers to think I could possibly do it." "Well", he said, "you could try".

I wrote a book which embodied all the questions that young people had asked me. They had taught me so much and made me think about how to answer these questions. Every answer led to more problems and more questions as you tried to apply them to individual situations. Finally, in 1956 I wrote a book called *Telling the Teenagers*. In those days 'teenagers' simply meant an age group – the teens, kids between thirteen and nineteen years old – during which a great many changes occur and a great many challenges confront adolescents. This book was addressed to teachers, youth leaders and social workers and there were very few books of that kind then. In fact, there was only one other book *Self Portrait of Youth* by Jordan and Fisher, which was about people in youth clubs who, as the Marriage Guidance Council had discovered, would rather talk themselves than be lectured to. Thus, I had great difficulty in finding a bibliography to put at the end of my book for further reading.

The circumstances were very different several years later when the

Marriage Guidance Council published a list of ninety titles about young people and teenagers. By then, of course, teenagers had become wealthy and were a source of money and a marketing target. It is amazing how the teenage market has grown: clothes, records, gadgets, pop concerts, an endless list. When I wrote my first book they never seemed to have any money at all to spend. They were either dependent on pocket money or were students with absolutely nothing to spend on the things they think necessary today. Young workers earned very little in those days. Now, in 1995, the pendulum has swung again and unemployed youngsters are poor.

When my book came out it was put on compulsory reading lists for people training in youth work and similar careers. One of the Child Care inspectors, a Miss Mawe at the LCC, said, "Really, you should adapt this book so that young people could read it". We were very concerned then that most of the child care workers were single women who were far too inhibited to talk about these matters to their charges. So she felt that perhaps we could find something that these young people might read for themselves. At just about that time paperbacks were coming into fashion.

My publisher suggested that I go to an agent. This agent introduced me to Pan Paperbacks who said they would publish this book if I revised it. They would publish it either for young people or for the original readers I had planned it for. Miss Mawe was very keen that I should do something for young people and accordingly I wrote this book for teenagers. Someone at Pan thought of the title, *The Opposite Sex*. I re-wrote *Telling the Teenagers* with the help of some of the young people with whom I was in contact.

Some of my young 'advisors' were in the care of the LCC and some I had met in Holloway Prison (where I had been working with Lady Jean Medawar). They were girls who had failed their probation period after a Borstal sentence and had been sent to Holloway Prison. At the time there were enlightened prison governors , such as Charity Taylor. Some of the officers were trained to do group work with these girls and various people came in to teach them different subjects. One of the social workers asked me to come in and run groups. I learned an enormous amount from these girls; whether they learned anything from me is a moot point.

They helped me a great deal in devising ways of writing this book, which ran into six printings and sold about a quarter of a million copies. Instead of being a substitute for giving talks, however, the book led to far more requests for lectures, meetings and conferences. I had a wonderful time. I do not know whether my husband enjoyed this period of my life so much. He retired quite young, in his sixties. I told him, "Well, you may be retired but I am not going to retire, stay at home and cook all day long. I'll cook one meal a day!" And so he entered into my career and was an enormous help and support. I went on to attend more and more conferences and lectures and sat on more and more committees.

Although I was in great demand as a speaker for Marriage Guidance, there was often a mixed reception. Very many groups and individuals were quite hostile. I was invited to speak at annual general meetings all over the country. In the chair there might be an embarrassed Mayor or other local dignitary who knew little or nothing about this new movement. Once I was introduced as the "Sexpert" and once defined as an "Xspurt" (i.e. 'X', the unknown quantity, and 'spurt', the drip under pressure!).

One youth club, at the request of parents, forbade the Youth Leader ever to invite me again because we had discussed masturbation. I had been a regular speaker and group leader at a Further Education Centre in Somerset where weekend education conferences were held for young workers and apprentices. When a new warden was appointed he decided that more outdoor activities should be on the programme and no more sitting around talking about sex.

Young people told me that parents had thrown my book into the fire or put it in the dustbin. Nevertheless, my popularity grew, especially after some radio or TV programmes. In many areas, 'Education for Personal Relationships' was encouraged in schools and youth clubs. Sex education is only a small part of such programmes. Our policy in Marriage Guidance was to deal with sex as part of the whole subject of gender, family relationships, friendships, love and marriage.

When I look back over nearly fifty years of these activities, it seems as if little progress has been made. Sex is often taught as a clinical activity, designed to provide relief from bodily urges while avoiding pregnancy and disease, although AIDS is emphasised more than VD and syphilis. Even such teaching is still the subject of argument and objection. Young people still prefer to talk about feelings, how to overcome shyness, develop confidence, make friends and find love, and how to cope with parents, siblings and authority figures. The facts about sex are soon explained and there are endless discussions and explicit videos and TV programmes about sexual techniques. I am still convinced, however, that two people exploring together individual feelings and ideas, actions and reactions, must always be unique and find their own ways to communicate and seek out the joy when love and sexual satisfaction are united in affectionate commitment. One can only hope that in spite of recession, setbacks and ignorant government ministers, a child's real needs for understanding will be met.

I met and became friends with many wonderful teachers and social workers and others and I followed their subsequent careers with great interest. In connection with Family Planning, I met some marvellous people: Lady Morag Bramley, Sylvia Dawkins, Beth Jacob, Faith Spicer, Rosalie Taylor and many others. And, of course, the pioneers of the Brook Clinics and Family Planning: Helen Brook, Augusta Landman, Jean Medawar, Margaret Pyke. They deserve to be mentioned and must not be forgotten.

* * *

The other activity which was a great interest of mine was mental health and community care. At the time of the 1959 Mental Health Act I was involved in the Mental Health Association which had been started by Lord Feversham. He thought that all groups interested in mental health should get together and pool their views and knowledge. The Feversham Committee developed into the National Association for Mental Health and now has branches all over the country under the name MIND.

After the 1959 Act everybody talked a lot about community care. Successive governments asked local authorities to prepare five-year and ten-year plans. Plans appeared in great abundance and they are still coming thick and fast from local Health Authorities and voluntary organisations but the money has never been forthcoming and the community care that we so carefully planned has been starved of funds and never come fully into operation. Valuable work has been done in this field by some forward-thinking local authorities and a few mental hospitals but now there is this anxious drive to close mental hospitals when there is still far too little community care. It is left to too few establishments run by local authorities and hospitals, and some provided by voluntary organisations such as MIND, the Schizophrenia Fellowship and so on.

I could write a great deal about mental health work but it all goes back to my early interest in people. Why is it that, when there is so much disaster, war, illness and trouble in the world, human beings add so much more to human suffering, through lack of satisfactory personal relationships? I would not go along with R D Laing who argues that all schizophrenia or mental illness is entirely due to family relationships going wrong. I maintain that there must be a great many other factors that we do not yet understand. For example, the fact that many people are able to survive in the community only because of drugs is something we ought to know a great deal more about – the chemistry of the brain and the body – as well as interpersonal relationships. It seems to me that very few people are studying either.

Incidentally, the only psychoanalyst who ever really applied psycho-analytical findings to body manifestations and body language was Wilhelm Reich, who was thrown out of the psychoanalytical group of his day and was gravely misunderstood. He died in an American prison. I still think we can learn a great deal from Reich's writings, as I believe in mind and body together. In recent years I have also come to see that the Alexander Technique of relaxation as enormously important. I have gained a great deal from Dr Wilfred Barlow's teaching, as well as from learning to do the Tai Chi Chuan exercises which link closely with Alexander in their ideas and origins. I would like to think that future therapists will deal with mind and body together and be far less narrowly specialised in their approach to problems.

Mark and I both worked for MIND in the Camden Association for Mental Health This was a voluntary movement which helped rehabilitate people who had spent long periods in mental hospitals or had breakdowns. I was on the management committee of Friern, the big mental hospital. Some of us were totally opposed to government decisions to close mental hospitals in North London unless other facilities were provided in the community.

The Mental Health Act of 1959 followed a Royal Commission and a White Paper which stated that large institutions were out of date and that people should be treated in the community, in their homes or in small establishments for day care as well as residential.

In the Greater London area there was no such provision so a few of us got together and started the Camden Association for Mental Health (very few of that group are still alive). We started by organising small groups and clubs, such as Sunday lunch for lonely people, and then we bullied the local Council into letting us have derelict houses on licence for fifty pence a week. A group of volunteers repaired and decorated them, collected money to install bathrooms, and we gradually built up a range of homes. Now there are sixty places in small group homes or flats without staff; or hostels, some with part-time help and some fully staffed. We built this up from nothing with grants from the Local Authority, the Health Service, Manpower Services Commission, and wherever else we could raise money. We established a full-time Day Centre which the Council then took over and that is still very successful. A second Day Centre opened in 1980 built on all the experience we had gained of what was needed. The centre opens every day and on Sunday for lunch, and some evenings and Saturdays for various activities. Volunteers have given place to paid staff and Camden MIND now employs forty four staff! Volunteers tend now to be 'helpers' or young people looking for jobs and adding some short-time experience to their CVs.

Mark had a major stroke in 1980 and was very ill and paralysed but, after a long period, he was able to walk a little with help. When the Day Centre was to be opened I had a nurse to help me and we managed to get Mark to the ceremony.

Lo and behold, the Mayor got up, declared it open and pulled a little curtain back from a plaque on the wall which announced: "The Rose and Mark Hacker Centre". We both nearly fainted! It was the best-kept secret. We'd been on the committee making all the plans and understood it was to be called the Camden Association for Mental Health. I was so shocked and excited I could hardly speak my acknowledgement. It was just a week before our Golden Wedding – what better present could one possibly have imagined!

Mark and me at the opening of the Day Centre

In some ways it seems just as well that Mark and the enthusiastic group of volunteers who planned and carried out this work are no longer alive to see the results of Government policies which have brought 'rate-capping', cuts in grants for charitable services and a general emphasis on cash rather than care. The Hacker Centre has gone. Camden MIND now has larger premises named Barnes House, where there are offices for each department of administrators.

* * *

I have some old diaries, which note only appointments, and dipping into them at random I find it hard to believe that I managed to do so much. Every day, even every minute, seems to be full! (Now, after an afternoon nap at eighty nine, I find everything too much trouble and hours go by wherein I have achieved so little and so slowly.)

In 1959, for example, I gave lectures or led discussion groups on sixty two occasions. These included schools, youth clubs, training colleges, universities, conferences of social workers, health visitors, several programmes on television and radio, summer schools, annual general meetings of Marriage Guidance Councils or mental health projects. A great deal of travelling was involved in such activities. Often I stayed overnight with other workers in these fields. A conference would last a weekend or a whole week. I made many lasting friendships and often one contact led to others.

In my diaries there are many references to living-in help. For some years it was Renata, an Italian who, after a few years, discovered that she could do less work and earn more money in a household that could afford more than one maid. Accordingly, she took herself off to Mayfair but not before she had recommended Hilda, who she had met at a linguists' club and who remained part of the family until she died. Hilda came from the area around the Baltic which meant that she was 'stateless' and had a Nansen passport. She had left Germany on political grounds and the rest of her family was in what was then the Eastern zone. She became devoted to my mother and often spent her free days with her. Hilda was brought up in a German children's home where those whose parents could not afford to pay had to act as servants to the children whose parents paid the fees.

Hilda's love for my mother brought back memories of her own mother and she finally visited East Germany, found her family and then continued to send her long-lost mother regular food parcels. Her brother came to stay with us, a doctor, so Hilda was no longer isolated. Eventually, when Mark retired and the boys had left home, we agreed that we did not really need a full-time resident housekeeper and, although still living with us, Hilda found and kept a job in a bank. Eventually she found a tiny flat of her own and we kept in touch.

Hilda died suddenly, alone in her flat, and although she made friends and was helpful to many of her neighbours, three days passed before anyone noticed that she had not been seen and the police were called. Our dear nurse Anneliese, who came to England from Germany before the war as a refugee and later resumed her teaching career, also died in her flat alone and was not found until the next day. It should be possible, but nowadays it is rare, to die in the arms of someone who cares for you.

With and without Hilda, I was out and about every day during this period. These old diaries note two or three half days each week when I would deal with Marriage Guidance cases at headquarters in London, Duke Street, and Harley Street or Islington or Camden, in Family Planning Clinics or CABs. There were many committee meetings at Friern Hospital and at the National Hospital for Nervous Diseases and other Health Authorities. Teaching hospitals were run by Boards of Governors which consisted of upper class people, mainly men, often titled and/or directors of large companies, with no local authority or staff representatives, certainly no union representatives. General and mental hospitals were run by Hospital Management Committees. There were fewer titles among the members and over the years representatives of the Local Authorities, political parties, trade unions and staff were appointed or co-opted, but Governors had greater freedom in allocating funds to various departments than HMCs.

I have watched enormous changes in the structure of the National Health Service and the gradual demoralisation of hospital staff as more and more bureaucracy took over and everything had to go 'through the proper channels'. Now staff have to care for more patients with fewer resources. In medical care and nursing there have been great advances in drugs and in treatment and there are often better attempts to communicate with patients and their relatives and more understanding of the whole person and of psychosomatic medicine. At the same time financial cuts and constant changes in Government policy make it more difficult to carry out improved methods of care, leading to stress at all levels.

Lawrence and friend

One day at a Health Authority meeting I thought, "Why am I here? I feel frustrated, bored, unhappy." For thirty years I had enjoyed the work and can look back on many improvements and innovations in which I played a part. Now I can take no pride in cuts and setbacks and endless plans that never come to fruition. So at age eighty, I resigned from this Health Authority and all other committees.

Over the years there have been so many changes but there seems to me to be a general loss of concern for the individual. We used to be a source of support to the staff as well as concerned with patients, pupils or children or old people in care. Now people have little time to give and voluntary concern has yielded place to paid professional supervisors, team leaders, organisers, and so forth.

* * *

Alongside all these public activities I was very busy with my happy family and social life: dinner parties, theatres, concerts, even opera at Glyndebourne until it became outrageously expensive. During these eventful years my boys became established in their careers and marriages. In 1960 Lawrence married Tessa and in 1963 Michael married Elisabeth. After ministering to the needs of three males for so long it was a delight to acquire two daughters-in-law. We have all kept very close as a family and both couples live nearby.

Sitting with Tessa, Lawrence's wife, in the garden at Highgate

It has been of great interest to me to compare the lives of modern women with my own. Both my daughters-in-law are gifted artistically and my home contains many examples of their work which give me much joy. Over the years I have vicariously enjoyed all the different kinds of work they have undertaken. Currently Tessa is writing and Elisabeth is training to be a counsellor. Unusual these days is the fact that both these marriages have lasted well over thirty years and now one of my grandsons is married.

In 1965 I was lecturing at Reading University to a group of teachers in training when a secretary brought me a note. My first grandson, Daniel, had arrived! His first days were spent in an incubator but he thrived and I shall never forget the feeling of ineffable joy when I was able to hold this little person. Whatever I write will seem absurd, sentimental, mawkish, but I know I have never experienced such bliss! In 1969 Elisabeth and Michael had another son, Jacob.

As Mark had retired about this time, we both fully enjoyed being grandparents. Elisabeth and Michael were only too glad to use us as babysitters. How different from my behaviour when my mother, equally happy to care for my children, had to abide by my strict written instructions as to what they were to do and eat and how they should be disciplined. Elisabeth was so grateful for a few hours or days of freedom and she allowed us to have fun with our grandsons in our own way.

Michael and ....

I have never forgotten how wonderful it was when they brought Danny to stay with us while

Elisabeth went into hospital to have Jacob. There they were in the hall, waiting for the ambulance. Elisabeth and Michael were panting together, doing one of the breathing exercises they had practised – the new father-to-be entering into the experience – eager to see the birth of their child and then to be partners in parenthood. So different from my time and my mother's when the men were excluded from the whole business and given the role of punisher and provider. Mark delighted in pushing the pram, was willing to help with changing and feeding after weaning. Later he enjoyed playing with them and teaching them to use tools. His grandsons brought him enormous pleasure. When I walk on the Heath I have so many happy memories of two generations of boys growing up – my sons and my grandsons. Flying kites, feeding the ducks, climbing trees, making and flying model planes, sailing model boats and, in winter, tobogganing and skiing down the hill, that I see from my windows. This is the beloved Heath where I walked with my father, oh, so long ago. There is still the meadow beside the Ladies Pond where I still swim, where grasses and wild flowers grow as high as I was then.

In spite of all our activities we had some wonderful holidays. We would set off in the car with maps and guidebooks and sometimes fixed destinations when we stayed with friends, often in Toulouse or Valbonne or Israel, only we flew there, hiring a car. Once, in Israel, Mark was unable to hire a car, being over seventy, so we took it in my name and he did most of the driving: one of his

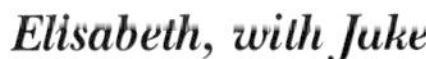

Elisabeth, with Jake

extremely rare illegal deeds! Our last two holidays before his illnesses were in a flat, lent to us by friends, on Lake Garda. Both times coincided with the opera season in Verona and we heard six operas in that uniquely wonderful setting.

We had many European friends. Our close friends in Toulouse deserve mention as we knew them very well and for a long time. Elsie's own story is strange. A good Catholic, she only discovered her origins when the Nazi invaders demanded proof of pure Aryan blood. Her mother had married an English Jew, divorced soon after her baby was born and re-married. Elsie was brought up a French Catholic and never told that she had had another father until papers had to be produced for the Germans.

They were active in the resistance and their home was a safe-house for escaping prisoners of war, air-crew, Jews and resistance workers. Eventually the Germans found out. By then one daughter had married an Englishman and one son had betrayed the family by acquiescing in his call-up by the Vichy Government. Her husband, a Professor of Electro-Chemistry, came to England, giving valuable aid to our war effort. Elsie and her four younger children had to run for their lives and spent a year in difficult circumstances in Portugal and Spain, eventually reaching England.

In Letchworth a French woman had organised "Les Amies des Volontaires Francaises" and some of us agreed to have the four children in the holidays so they could be together. Different boarding schools had them in term time. Elsie was actively campaigning in England for help for Resistance activists. Her English was perfect and she was an excellent speaker. She was a wonderful friend, warm and affectionate and amazingly intelligent: one of my many role models and mother substitutes. Maurice was our holiday guest, a beautiful lad, and he and Michael became close friends.

Back in France, after the war, they were given a newly-built house on the campus of the University of Toulouse and many a good time we enjoyed there. Maurice was a conscript in the colonial wars and survived Dien Bien Phu only to be shot in the back by the French Algerians in Toulouse, while pasting up posters urging the election of de Gaulle. Elsie came to stay with me at this time as the commiserations and condolences of all the University people were too overwhelming. The family had other ghastly tragedies. The recalcitrant son forgiven by his mother but never by his father, was killed in a car crash. The remaining son (there were originally three boys and three girls), the only one to carry on the family name, became a Depute and his wife produced five daughters. At last the longed-for boy was born but, at about eighteen months old, fell out of a window and died. I flew to Toulouse to stay for a short while. Why do such things happen so often to wonderful people who deserve better from fate?

We enjoyed some exciting events in Toulouse. I have vivid memories of their Golden Wedding and the time when public officials came from Paris to award the Rosette for the Legion d'Honneur. At these times the whole campus was en fete and all the grandchildren lined up in their best clothes, all the little girls in white. One time so many were staying with the family that Mark and I took a room in a hotel in Toulouse. On the day of the party, the farmers staged a protest. The town centre was surrounded with tractors preventing any traffic movement. We phoned our plight and, lo and behold, two members of the faculty, former Resistance workers, rescued us, persuading us to walk in front of a tractor and risk the hooting and swearing until we dodged down a side street where they had hidden a car

From Counsellor to Councillor

The Negative Capability:
When a man is capable of being in
uncertainties, mysteries, doubts,
without any irritable reaching
after fact and reason.
John Keats

The year 1973, like 1951, was a major turning point in my life. Counselling, teaching, lecturing and writing books for over twenty five years had been enormously satisfying. During this period, however, every aspect of my life changed. My sons had left home and my husband had retired. Although he was able to support me in many ways, my work began to intrude on our partnership.

At the age of sixty five I retired from counselling. The Marriage Guidance Council had long before decided upon this retirement age. In the commercial world a retirement age is fixed. In voluntary work it is more difficult for colleagues to decide whether or not a worker is suitable for responsible work. Hence our decision to make it mandatory to retire at sixty five. I certainly did not feel, in 1971, that I was anything but competent and skilled and I continued to teach and run training groups for several years after retirement.

My work had taught me so much and had enriched my life in many spheres. I believe that I helped many people, not only as individuals or in their family and sex life, but also in their careers. It had been a great joy to see people 'take off' where I ended and incorporate the ideas of relationships, pioneered by the Marriage Guidance Council, into the fields of education, social work, nursing and so on.

It was painful indeed to retire and I missed especially the group work and the interesting people all over the country furthering our aims and ideals.

What was I to do now that 'old age' stared me in the face?

I remembered my trip to Russia in 1932 when I talked to Beatrice Webb about Marx and Freud and whether to work as a politician or a social worker. I remembered that shrewd old campaigner looking at me and saying: "Social work for you?!" I wondered if she had summed me up correctly. I had chosen and been well rewarded; now I saw a chance to develop the more assertive and exhibitionist facets of my character.

In 1971 I had the opportunity to choose again. There was a call for nominations for candidates for the Greater London Council (GLC). Someone proposed me. Why not, I said to myself recklessly and I agreed to my name being put forward. After a lifetime of Labour Party activity, including countless periods of canvassing for others, it was strange to be knocking on doors and making speeches saying, "Vote for me". Shortly afterward, to my surprise and pleasure, I found myself the elected member for the constituency of St Pancras North in the Borough of Camden. From 1973 to 1977 I spent an incredible four years in public service despite Mark's increasing illness.

As a counsellor I had developed my listening, receptive, empathic roles. As a therapist, one's aggressions are inhibited, one's instinctual likes and dislikes concealed behind a facade of interest and concern and not just a facade, for one must truly be interested and concerned, and there must be at least an element of caring – if not loving.

I have often spoken of a life-long conflict within myself. If one wants to use some of one's energies to make the world less miserable (or is this a self-delusion, too, and one's motives are very far from altruistic, but spring from the deep unconscious), what is the best way to go about it? Should one do one's mite to help individuals or relieve pain and suffering as one finds opportunities? Should one devote all one's efforts to good causes? Should one cultivate one's garden? Or should one work on the political front to change society?

So here I was at County Hall in 1973, the sixty seven year old member for St Pancras North, entering the political arena in a new way. What a challenge! At that time, the Greater London Council was the intermediate layer of government between the local boroughs and the national government. It was based on constituencies co-terminous with those electing MPs. After a period in opposition the Labour Party was in power from 1973 until 1977, when the Tories gained control again. I had been at County Hall earlier, as a co-opted member of the Children's Committee, when it had been the London County Council. This time, however, I was there as an elected member and had my own seat in the Council Chamber.

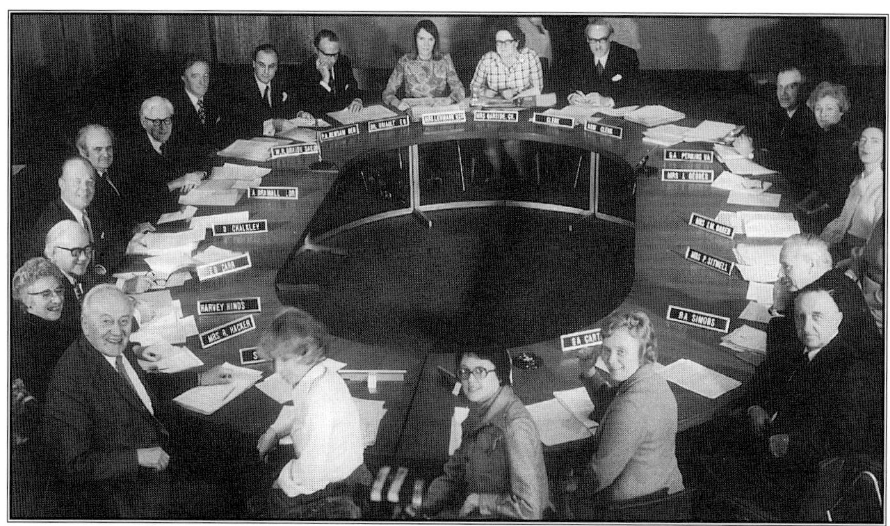

I was on a great many committees because, not having a paid job, it was assumed that I had more time so, between these committees and running my own family and a great many other things, I was fully occupied! I was appointed chairman of a small but, as it turned out, a most important sub-committee called Thames and Other Waterways Board. One of my main election themes was "Don't let the Tories Ruin London". At that time they wanted only office blocks and hotels and anything to make money for entrepreneurs, whereas the Labour Party campaigned for more public housing and more amenities for the people of London. Among the London waterways are a lot of tributaries which lead into the Thames as well as the Thames itself. For these we planned public walkways and parks and water sports and amenities instead of private access from hotels and offices. There had even been threats to fill in all the canals and make them into roads, which we thought would ruin London. Generally the scope of the Thames and Other Waterways Board was quickly enlarged beyond the small sub-committee framework originally mapped out for it.

This was some of the most exciting work I have ever done. I loved it and I loved the public attention given to my vision. I think some of this came through in an article by Dennis Barker in *The Guardian* (July 31, 1976), entitled "River Dream of Mrs Hacker" in which he said: "Mrs Rose Hacker, I insist, is not mad. She visualises a River Thames which is a positive tourist attraction and aesthetic amenity for rich and poor but still I say she is not mad. A visionary perhaps."

I wanted a clear view of Southwark Cathedral from the river, a system of land 'fingers' to the water all down the river, a pier for river-borne arrivals at the National Theatre and the Royal Festival Hall and a maritime museum with machinery and ships.

I believed that the Thames should have national funding and coordinated planning. I wanted to see teams of volunteers to clean it up. I tried a few schemes but the unions would object because they had cut down on staff to clear the rubbish. There was a British invention of a small boat that could pick up rubbish and at the same time skim oil from the surface and re-claim it. But no-one had the money to do anything like that.

There were other obstacles to our vision of the Thames. There was nothing in the Water Bill about land. What were you supposed to do to get to the water   use a helicopter? We had to fit in with other people's various plans because we owned practically no land. It had to be agreed by persuasion. I wanted a bigger maritime museum to preserve some of the dockland machinery and actual ships but when you thought of a nice place for it, you found it was in the hands of private owners who were developing it for profit.

It was wonderful to have some power to put "my vision" into reality. We did do a lot of work on changing the waterways at this time. We supported clubs and marinas for young and old. We promoted the cleaning of the canals, making walks along the canal towpaths and developing the markets and shopping centres like the Camden Lock and the Portobello. Painting the bridges over the Thames, developing extra small parks, providing seating and open spaces along the river, building and repairing what already existed were among our achievements.

I was also on the Transport Committee. We instituted the idea of free fares for old age pensioners and disabled people. We had lots of ideas and policies for reducing the cars in London and having more public transport but vested interests made them difficult to implement. We were also doing a great deal to promote public housing for rent but that was all abolished by a later Conservative Government and GLC.

Then there were all the Education Committees, covering over one thousand schools. The big transformation through the establishment of comprehensive schools took place during this period – a true revolution in education. At that time there were tremendous differences between the various kinds of education available. There was the 'eleven plus' examination which was intended to 'separate sheep from goats'. Those who passed went to grammar schools and the others went to secondary modern schools. If you went to a grammar school, you had a better chance of higher education or white collar employment. From a secondary modern school you were unlikely to receive any further academic education after the age of fifteen or sixteen. During my time on the ILEA the 'eleven plus' system was abolished in London.

The other great revolution was in special education, which also interested me. I had been a member of committees set up in 1948 when the National Health Service was instituted. At that time there were big institutions for handicapped children – hydrocephalic, big swollen heads – children with multiple handicaps and very little individual care. One would see large wards full of children in cots rocking and banging their heads. There weren't enough staff to mother them. In 1971 an Act was passed, however, to create schools for the 'severely sub-normal'. Before that they were deemed 'ineducable'. Now we had schools for mildly sub-normal children, just as we had schools for the deaf, the blind, the delicate and physically handicapped children. This was the beginning of a new concept; instead of labelling children, you spoke rather of 'learning or physical difficulties' and dealt with them. At the present time the education revolution is continuing to try to integrate these children with the so-called 'normal' children. However, with limited financial resources, this may be a backward step.

In the 1970s there was a growing horror of big mental institutions. Instead we established schools (I was chair of one of the first of them) instead of merely occupational centres for the severely handicapped. Stanley Segal, a headmaster, wrote *No Child is Ineducable*, and this is true, given sufficient well-trained staff. Instead of separating children, we said that all children should attend the same schools and that the school must provide comprehensive education where the right curriculum could be devised for each child.

A school prizegiving

You may have mixed ability teaching. Do you stream the children or give them individual time-tables in separate groups? You get more segregation and discrimination when you put children into separate streams in a big school. Mixed ability teaching has to be very well done to succeed. The comprehensive ideal is a good ideal but it hasn't always been successful. It is still true that children from good homes – where there are books and parents who encourage them – have a much better chance. How do you give other kids a better chance? So many children are disadvantaged through poverty, unemployment and ill health. We now live in a multi-cultural society. I think there are about fifty languages spoken in London schools. So how do you give all children a fair chance? It is so difficult to know what to do but we must reform our educational system if we are to change our society. Alas, since Thatcher and the abolition of the GLC and ILEA, many special schools have been closed and progressive ideas are out of fashion.

* * *

All this time Mark was wonderfully supportive. He had learned to cook his own meals when I was out and he would often meet me at County Hall. His support was crucial. He was always ready to take me and fetch me from far-away meetings and we had wonderful holidays together, exciting adventures and new experiences with which he co-operated fully. Having no children at home and having passed the menopause gives women a new lease of life. It is important of course to keep healthy and that is not always within one's own powers, but I was fortunate in this respect and had plenty of energy.

I learned a great deal in my role as Chair of Thames and Other Waterways. It is amazing how much knowledge one can amass quickly in the course of new duties for which one needs to be well supported, and the support was always there at County Hall. I had an office, I had secretaries, I had the use of the knowledge of many skilled and well qualified officers for the subjects in which I was interested. It is regrettable that the GLC no longer exists with its expertise, its libraries, its archives and the many people always willing to help and advise.

Alongside all this public activity, there was the joy of seeing my two sons happily married and my two grandsons growing up, all living quite near and

Danny and Jake, sons of Michael and Elisabeth

Danny's wife, Victoria

visiting very often. The pleasures of family are a nourishment when one is active outside the home. It is the balance of a life where love, affection and support are vitally important, especially as women move more into active life outside the home. I have so often seen the effect of putting too much strain on marriage and family life. Quite often one is sacrificing one aspect of one's life for another and the balance is more easily reached with a co-operative partner. This is why I am so convinced that we must re-educate men and think far more about the roles of men and women and the stereotypes that have to be broken and changed. Single men and women also need support when leading stressful lives.

* * *

Suddenly Mark became ill for the first time before I began at County Hall. This protracted illness continued through this exciting period of my life in the GLC. One night in 1968 I came home to find him in terrible pain. We sent for a doctor immediately and the subsequent X-ray showed that he had a stoppage of the bowel and pancreatitis. He was in hospital for a week during which many tests were taken, while he grew weaker and weaker. They did not operate and the bowel stoppage finally corrected itself of its own accord, leaving him totally dehydrated. He could hardly lift his hand to brush his hair. I had to look after him like a baby until he recovered. I think it took about a year before he recovered his strength.

I remember a holiday in Amalfi when Mark could do very little and had to be supported even to walk; but he recovered and came to terms with this. Then he had a terrible pain in his leg. This turned out to be Buerger's or Smokers' disease – a blocked leg artery which makes walking very painful. After about five or ten minutes there is intolerable pain and one has to rest. This meant an end to all activities like long walks, gardening, skiing and so on. Mark felt this very keenly: he suffered a depressive breakdown and simply couldn't bring himself to do anything except think about the possibilities of gangrene, of losing his leg. He refused any psychiatric treatment or drugs for this depression which lasted about three months. He always felt that he could deal with all difficulties himself; he had done so from childhood onwards, when he held himself responsible for his father's unemployment and for the family's poverty, and set out to do something to remedy these troubles.

It was galling and very difficult indeed for him to accept any kind of dependence. I, too, was not very happy about having to do so much for him, having accepted him always as helper and supporter. Gradually he came to terms with his lack of activity and he still tried to do as much as he could, accompanying me to many of my meetings and outings. However, one day he became very upset and angry. He lost his temper with me, describing many resentments that he had kept hidden. Perhaps I should have realised how much he was sacrificing for me, but I didn't. I was too happy, accepting all he did and enjoying my life to the full.

I decided after this outburst that I would never leave him overnight and I would do as much as I could to involve him more in things that I was doing. He was very willing to go along with this and relieved at not being left alone at night. I think he was rather frightened of being ill and of not being able to cope with pain, but then it was rather like Job – as fast as he got used to one illness and learned to cope, he got another.

One day he got a fly or something in his eye and, as he closed it, he realised that he couldn't see out of the other eye at all. He had only peripheral sight, with darkness across the centre of vision. Nobody could say when this had happened but it turned out to be nothing to do with his eyes, but again to do with the blood circulation, hardening of the arteries, probably due to smoking. (He'd been a heavy smoker all his life and, although he smoked a bit less when people became aware of the dangers, he never gave it up, except for one short period just to prove his control over himself.)

When we learnt about the cause of this eye trouble we were very alarmed indeed. The specialist who assumed, quite rightly, that Mark was an intelligent person, warned him that the other eye might go the same way, insisting that if he had any trouble at all with his eyes he was to come back to Moorfields Hospital immediately. We never really decided what 'immediately' meant, but at that point Mark decided he would never go away on a holiday again and would not like to be far from Moorfields. This meant that, for the last eight years of Mark's life, we were always in London.

I think, when one has all these illnesses, the fear is often very much worse than the illness itself. We do need to be trained to cope with the fear that comes with illness and with the lack of independence that often accompanies it. There is a vast need to train people for old age, to cope with illness and to be a carer of a dependent and sick relative. These are roles which are very difficult indeed and which many people – in fact most people – may pass through in the course of a long life. Not enough is done to appreciate this, to prepare for these roles. Carers themselves have banded together to demand more help and support because there are millions who are saving the country vast sums of money by caring for sick relatives at home.

It is important – and I have been fortunate all my life, mainly through various activities – to find new and younger friends who are a great joy as one gets older and loses old and dear friends. There is a problem however. I find myself becoming more selfish and preferring to spend time with young, lively companions, rather than going to sit with those who are physically disabled or who find it too difficult to communicate because their minds are rambling. Trying to communicate with somebody who is deaf is very disturbing and painful and – let me confess – boring, even though these are people one has loved for many years. So there is always a conflict between being kind and being selfish and enjoying pleasures that are still available and that one feels may not be there for much longer because of one's advancing years. One feels, "well, maybe I will be senile, deaf, blind, unable to communicate, and who will then come and see me?" And this makes one selfish about the present.

But there are many compensations. One has to find inner resources, find pleasures alone and not always be seeking for other people to be helpful or interesting or companionable. I find more and more I can enjoy my own company and not feel too miserable when the days go by and nobody telephones, visits or writes. But then there is the joy when you realise that there are still some people around with whom you are mutually companionable and can share interests and activities. I am fortunate, too, in that I have many friends that I have known for a very long time, mainly women, although there are still a few old men around with whom I can share happy memories and I have tried to cultivate a mixed group of friends.

When I was in Letchworth I was a member of the Luncheon Club. The motto was, "The only way to have a friend is to be one" and I have never forgotten this. Friendships must be kept in good repair. If one can't visit, one can telephone or write, but there are people who live on modest pensions for whom even the telephone bills are frightening. More should be done to help old people to keep in some kind of communication with others.

I feel a certain amount of disillusionment these days. It began with the great shock of the rise of Fascism, with the realisation that people are not very rational and the irrational is still far too powerful. When you look at the world of nuclear bombs and the pollution of our own environment, you can see that the world is ma, and sanity is in short supply. We have to cherish the sane bits but we have to realise all the time that the world is not divided into sane people and mad. We are all both mad and sane, rational and irrational: it's a question of balance. We all have to develop our potential to the full and it's when we are full of frustration that we feel anger and bitterness and depression. We tend to think it's always someone else's fault but the fault is often in ourselves. We've got to see what's wrong with us and try to change ourselves and that is particularly important for men. We've got to alter the thinking of men much more now. Women have made some progress but not enough or, rather, the thinking has been done but it hasn't been put into effect.

Women are still at a disadvantage. They still don't earn the same wages. We still don't get men taking their full role in the home and sharing the children. Men feel they're doing the woman a favour when they do a bit in the house. We have to change this, to share everything according to our own potential. If you like looking after children, whether you're a man or a woman, look after children. If you want to be ambitious and go out and do something, you should be able to do this. But it's a very difficult thing to change role models, particularly for men. The development of their so-called feminine qualities which would give men greater strength, they see as weakness. Many men are afraid of women today. Women are changing and this is terrifying to men. A woman today may have succeeded in a career, gained confidence in herself as a whole person and feel that she has no need to be dependent on a man to keep her.

It was different in the past. I was a kept woman! In marriage sending the wife out to work was a disgrace. Your husband earned the money and you were Mrs Solicitor or Mrs Doctor or Mrs Coalminer or whatever. You took on a persona because of your husband's job and your husband's income. But many girls today earn far more than their boyfriends and what can the man offer them? Nothing.

It's very frightening to a man because women are sexually and economically liberated. One may have a chosen sex life, with lovers of either sex, and even children by artificial insemination. So what has marriage to offer? Yet many women have this longing for children that I think comes from the womb so with all the equality we are different. Women are like vessels for enfolding and enclosing and nurturing whereas men have physical attributes which are outgoing and extroverted. There is this longing of the body for nurturing and this leads you astray because not every woman enjoys being a mother. It seems that an innate need to care for a child, a lover, a husband, a parent, is part of the need for close companionship. To care and be cared for is a desire that may persist all through life and become stronger in old age, whether one is a man or a woman.

Looking back now, I recognise that being a mother as well as a wife seemed to drain all of my energies and attention. Although I had help in the early days, during the war there had been no help. At times I could have thrown my children out of the window. It's so boring day after day and night after night. Sometimes the kids are crying in the night, or you are up all night because they are ill, or they play up when you want to go out. You feel this is no life at all, whatever its joys and its constructive side. Certainly it is delightful to watch children growing up, to play with them and help them to become loving and intelligent adults. It is the most important and creative job anyone can ever do and men can be just as good at it. Looking back over a long life now, however, it seems that only a small part of one's life time is spent caring for children.

* * *

I still believe in socialism, and I don't believe in revolution because I don't believe in power as an end in itself. You have to have power to do anything, and I've enjoyed power, the bits that I've had. If you have no power you can achieve nothing, but power corrupts. All through history, whenever there has been a revolution, people have become mad with power and their enemies stage a coup and take over and are equally corrupt. This is going on in the world all the time. Madmen are taking over in too many countries. They want to carry out the ideals that they started out with, but the power for its own sake replaces the ends they sought. The ends do not justify the means and means are ends.

I think we need new ideas. I haven't lost sight of the need to nationalise. I believe you should nationalise land, banks, insurance and public utilities. But by 'nationalisation' I don't mean state capitalism. I mean participation of the people, for the people, by the people. That is what democracy is all about; but how to achieve it is the real problem. Things that have happened in the Eighties and Nineties have set the Labour Party back a long way, and we have to re-think and re-build. I'm sure we will do this, because I still believe that the human race cannot survive unless we work for a just society. If we don't feed the hungry we are doomed because, with present international communications, we live in one world. It must be a just world, because people won't tolerate starvation when others have too much luxury. One year's expenditure on armaments would solve all the problems in the Third World. I believe we need to find ways of achieving more equality. And by 'we' I mean the Labour Party.

The Conservative government succeeded in its aims: to weaken the unions and local government, to undermine the Welfare State and force privatisation. I am not against home ownership but the majority of people's wages won't run to paying off a mortgage. We still need a great deal of public housing for rent as there is too much exploitation by private landlords. The Conservative government sold shares in nationalised industries that the people already owned. They were bought out of rates and taxes, and selling them to the people who already own them through the State seems to me immoral.

People who might have been Labour are now being induced to think that they are capitalists. They find out when they're unemployed and they can't pay off the mortgage, they don't own their house at all. It is evil when property gives too much power over other people's lives. I used to be totally opposed to inherited wealth but I'm not so sure about that now I have grandchildren. I've inherited a little from my father and my husband which helps my children and grandchildren. But how far can one go? When it becomes the kind of wealth in the hands of a few that can control Third World countries, the power to promote Agribusiness in poor communities, to grow tropical fruit for export while the people starve, their forests and lands are destroyed or polluted, and a few grow rich. Capitalism moves into the Third World, not helping the people to feed themselves but exploiting them for profits.

I still believe in the Welfare State and progress through education, enlightenment and political action. But now I am no longer certain about the means to achieve this. We know we need a more just world, and that we must get rid of nuclear weapons. We know nations have to work together, and that we must eliminate the crippling debts of the Third World so they can feed themselves and develop their countries in their own way – not Coca Cola and hamburger style. People are waking up to this. The Empire has gone but we haven't begun to accept the implications of One World. Ecology is growing in importance, but where is the wisdom to make good use of modern technology? Huge, multinational companies have more power than national governments: no-one has yet devised methods of curbing their power and that of money markets and stock exchanges to make or break nations and institutions worldwide.

There have been so many changes in my lifetime, particularly of attitudes. As a child and young adult, I was very much aware of the impact of British imperialism in India and elsewhere. Later I had a lot of sympathy with Gandhi and the Indians who were trying to get their independence. It seemed to me monstrous the way people were exploited all over the world. I remember my uncle who was in the Civil Service discussing the 'natives' and he said, "Well, you treat them like children!" I once asked my aunt about the life of the Indian people. She described vividly the wealth and homes of the Maharajahs, the balls and banquets and garden parties, then she ended with an offhand comment, "You don't go near the native quarters – too smelly – but you can train the 'boys' and 'bearers and ayahs' (nannies) to be good servants". This conversation would be unthinkable today. Yet the exploitation continues in different ways through economic factors, the promotion of warfare and the sale of arms. If human beings do not wake up in time and change attitudes, we shall perish with a bang through nuclear war or accidental explosions, or with a whimper as pollution gradually poisons.

Alone but not Lonely

And what was it that I delighted in,
But to love and be loved?
But I kept not the measure of love,
Of mind to mind, friendship's bright boundary.
Saint Augustine

Adapting to widowhood and being alone is something for which we are never prepared. As a friend once said, the two worst things one has to face are coming home to an empty house and realising that one will never again be the most important person in someone else's life.

In 1983, a year after Mark died, I sold our large house on Highgate West Hill and bought a small flat, just behind where I had lived with Mark for thirty years. I wanted to stay in the neighbourhood, but realised that I needed to create (for financial but also for psychological reasons) a new environment for myself – one in which my beloved Mark had never lived – if I was to succeed in becoming, slowly and painfully, a new and single person.

It was difficult to give up my home, as I had become attached to my possessions and 'beloved objects'. It was difficult to be ruthless and give away or get rid of furniture, pictures, books, ornaments, treasures that have sentimental connotations, things that have been acquired together as a couple or given as presents by loved relatives or friends. Nevertheless, I am glad to have moved. My little flat is overcrowded but it is easy to look after. One can turn the key and go out or go away without worrying about too many things to keep clean or a big garden to care for.

Because I sold my house and moved into a flat with the mortgage paid, I now had money to spend on holidays. Indeed I felt I owed myself the holidays I had missed: for eight years I had not had a day off during Mark's illness.

Mark had become extremely dependent on me. It's only since he's gone that I realise how much he supported me earlier on and how much I depended on him. It was so hard to see his whole personality changing with the suffering. His demands upon me made me realise that I had been pretty selfish and indulged for many years. He changed gradually but completely and became like a demanding baby. His pain and the illness made him unable to give me anything back. That was what was so tragic.

I became exhausted. One can understand the battered baby syndrome, reaching a point of utter exhaustion with nothing left to give and yet having to keep giving on and on and on. I had never really understood that before. I felt I had to give but I had no resources to give so I felt guilty. I couldn't give what was expected and what was needed. This created an emotional conflict inside me but I was able to talk to someone about it. I've been so lucky because I was trained as a counsellor and not only was I able to face some of the awful things in myself but I had people I could turn to and with whom I could talk.

Even with hindsight those times still seem terrible. Being a nurse is a very demanding job. There are so many people in this position, having to be a nurse twenty four hours a day. I was fortunate in that I could afford help and, after talking to people who understood, I did something which changed my whole outlook about money. We'd always been rather careful and, as an accountant, Mark thought that Capital was sacred and never to be spent. We'd saved up, bought a house, paid off all the mortgage and were living reasonably in a secure sort of way. Then, talking to somebody, I realised this is utterly absurd when you're old. My children had said to me, "You don't have to leave it to us". So I thought, well, how long have we got? Let's just spend what we've got and mortgage the house, borrow, it didn't matter. As soon as I got that into my mind that money didn't matter, I could pay for help for Mark. I didn't have to send him away to hospital.

I was so lucky to have the resources. But at times I got so despairing that I said to myself, about Mark, "I wish you would die!" That made me feel terribly guilty. He kept saying, "I wish I could die" but he didn't want to take his own life. He wouldn't join EXIT and he hadn't shared my views about suicide when we were both well. He wouldn't discuss dying and he didn't really want to die. I got some advice and guidance about these terrible feelings that I hated in myself. I was able to talk about it and express what I saw as the full evil blackness of my soul. This is the essence of counselling, isn't it? That you can say these things to somebody with whom you feel safe and you know they won't say, "Oh, what a terrible person!" because they know there are the opposite feelings in you as well. People have to accept the black and white of their own souls. You have to find a way of expressing aggression and resentment. If you can't express it verbally, or even if you can, I think it's very good to express it physically through vigorous exercise, art, gardening, singing or playing an instrument.

It was strange how I felt when Mark actually died because he died so beautifully. That was the most extraordinary experience because he had been having a terrible time for months and months. One day he just said, "Oh, I want to go to sleep, I want to go to sleep" and we put him to bed. By that time it took two people to move him and lift him from chair to wheelchair, from wheelchair to bed. We put him to bed very early in the afternoon, which was something he'd never wanted to do. With me holding him like a baby, he said, "Oh, I want to go to sleep, I want to go to sleep. Don't leave me." It was very moving and so beautiful that I didn't feel sad until after he had died that afternoon.

I was then alone, but the realisation took a long time. When it came, my children, my sister Sally and my friends were wonderful, so I wasn't left alone. But still the fact that he wasn't there...I couldn't really believe it. He was there, really, until I moved. I felt he was in that house. That's why I had to move.

The move to my new flat was a complete metamorphosis in the circumstances of life. I've seen so many people hang onto their homes and their possessions and then they can't manage. Everything gets dirtier and more burdensome, more and more worrying and too expensive. I thought, "well, I won't be like that, I'd better move while I'm still able".

Because Mark was so full of encouragement and wanted to know all about the various activities that I did, I missed him enormously. This is the awful thing – that you come into an empty place and there's nobody there. We always talked about everything together. I realise that I thought I'd led a very independent life but in reality I had shared everything with Mark. He would comfort me and turn tears to laughter when I met with envy, rivalry, spite and rejection.

I still have lots of activities. I am still full of ideals and enthusiasm. But I do find I have to make myself do things. I can so well understand why widows go downhill. You think, "Why bother to get dressed, why bother to do anything, there's no focus to my life." On the other hand, you realise that you are alone but that there's a sense of freedom and liberation in that now you can do anything you want to do. However, you don't want to do it. At least, I find I don't really care very much whether I do it or not, but I do make myself have a full programme in order to survive. It would be very easy to go the other way.

Mark's death hasn't changed my philosophy of life. I fear death even less now but I do fear suffering and dependence. I'm more religious in a way than before, not in the conventional sense, but I do think there's a tremendous power of loving. I've had so much from people who've wanted to help me that one feels kind of supported in a very strange way.

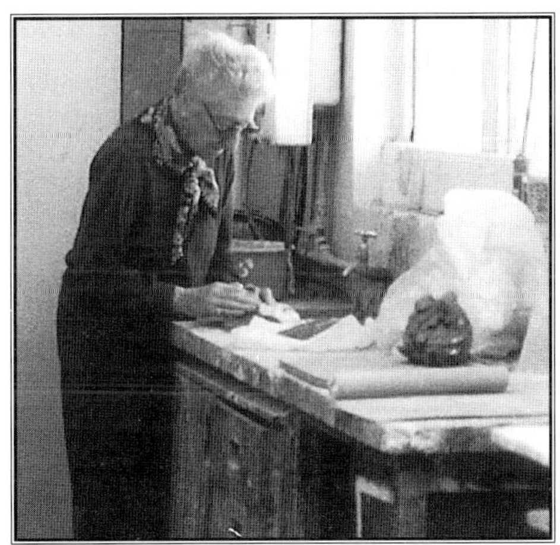

At work in the studio

I started to attend classes in sculpture. These were a great relief to me when Mark was so ill. Friends would sit with him and twice a week I would go to my class. That was a great joy. I understand even more now how people express themselves through creativity, and, of course, everybody can. London is so full of opportunities, except if you're not mobile! But people don't realise their potential. They can model, they could paint, but they just lament, "Oh, I'm old, oh, I'm a widow, nobody wants me". Well, I try to face that. I have a wonderful time when people ask me to go and stay with them, even if they are working. Often I have a lot of time to be alone. I've realised that I'm absolutely free to do whatever I like. I've never had that feeling in my life before, that there isn't anybody waiting for me to go home, or cook a meal or make tea. Nobody needs you and so you're quite free. But the other side of that coin is that nobody cares either! It doesn't matter whether you're there or not.

I am still alive and fairly well, although I have to take some medication. I am definitely enjoying life rather more. I don't feel impelled to serve on committees and save the world and fill every unforgiving minute! I doze off frequently and can enjoy being alone in my warm and comfortable flat. Fortunately I am still to be able to move, to see and to hear – however far from perfectly! – and to live amid green surroundings.

It took about four years after Mark's death to adjust to living alone and finding compensation for his companionship, with its pain at the end, after so many years of pleasure. During this period I had other reasons for depression. Too many of the good causes, for which I had striven so long and so diligently, were being rubbished. Among these were: Hallewick Hospital, a therapeutic community for the mentally ill; Shephall Manor, a boarding school for delinquent and unmanageable boys; Holly Court School, a school for children of all ages with learning difficulties; the Cockpit Theatre, a space for the arts in education and the community; Thames and other Waterways, the GLC committee which I chaired, designed to promote amenities for all on the water and waterside of rivers and canals.

The advent of Thatcherism seemed to have reversed the ethos of society. What was considered essential became merely frills or unnecessary unless paid for over a few years. Totally disillusioned and upset at committee meetings concerned mainly with cost-cutting, I resigned from all of them. I found new interests in my eighties, inspired in part by my visits to California.

* * *

When I was in the depths of bereavement, I had a letter from Moira Roth. Moira was the daughter of my friend Eve, who had so wonderfully taken us in as evacuees during the war. Eve had died in 1980 and I had spent a lot of time helping her in her last years.

Although Moira had spent most of her adult life in America, we had kept in touch and I had always felt that she was part of my family. Now a mature woman and a renowned art historian and critic, Moira was teaching art history at the University of California, San Diego. In 1982 she wrote to me to say, "What

Moira

you need now is a daughter and I need a mother. Come to California." I accepted this invitation with alacrity and shortly afterwards spent six weeks in this wonderful place, La Jolla, near San Diego.

Moira had no relatives at all and no children. She had been married and divorced and neither of us had been really close to our mothers. It was easy to work at an artificial mother/daughter relationship and this we have sustained over thirteen years, not difficult when we only meet for short periods once a year. To me this has been not only a joy and a consolation but a source of inspiration and new interests.

I have travelled to California almost every year since the mid-Eighties and have met many of Moira's friends. I obtained a liberal education in American feminism and met artists, writers, critics, coming back every year stimulated and re-educated. American feminists, especially Moira's friends, had moved from the vituperative, man-hating and aggressive mood of the early Seventies and had progressed towards a wider view and sound feminist scholarship. Some of them are writing about ancient civilisations (archaeology) where the goddess was worshipped.

Through Eve's books which she left when she died I first learned about Buddhism. Later, a friend of Eve's introduced me to Tai Chi. Over the years, I have found the link between Alexander Technique of Relaxation and Tai Chi. Now through Jo Hanson, a sculptor friend of Moira's, I have become deeply interested in the Goddess Culture. Books such as *The Chalice and the Blade* by Riane Eisler, *The Once and Future Goddess* by Elianor Gadon, *The Myth of the Goddess* by Anne Baring and Jules Cashford, *The Tao of Physics* by Fridof Capra, *The Tibetan Book of Living and Dying* by Sogyal Rimpoche, *Ageless Body, Timeless*

Mind by Deepak Chokra and many others, have widened the paradigms of my thinking. Historically, from considering 500 BC as a great turning point in world beliefs, I now focus on 5,000 BC and earlier. Through these studies, I have gained some clues toward accepting ageing and death.

Thus, over the last ten years, I have become obsessed with ancient history and this new perspective in which the worship of the male and the notion of God rather than the goddess seems quite recent history. My ideas about the need for the liberation of the male and the cultivation of the two sides of the brain and the need for closer communication between men and women have become increasingly central to my understanding of the world. In my recent sculpture I have found the goddess theme and the symbol of the snake intruding insistently. These ideas have been important to me in trying to become a whole person, able to live alone and not feeling lost and helpless without a male partner.

* * *

Although I cannot bring myself to worship a God or take part in religious rites, I have a deep regard for many sincere theologians and have been privileged to collaborate with distinguished scholars on training for pastoral care and marriage guidance. Among Christians, Reverend Gordon Dunstan and Canon Verney have inspired me. Rabbi Dov Marmur of Reform Judaism, now in Canada, was a great teacher. It was Rabbi Marmur who once invited me to deliver a sermon at the Alyth Gardens Synagogue in 1979, three years before Mark died.

In my childhood only men could take part in the synagogue. At that time, on very solemn occasions, men belonging to the tribe of the Cohens would ascend to the *Bima* (pulpit) and bless the congregation. Those belonging to the tribe of the Levites would attend to the preliminary washing of the hands. My father would leave his seat and go outside to prepare the Cohanim for this blessing. This ceremony was very important in emphasising the superiority of the male and especially those belonging to these important tribes.

When Hitler came to power in the 1930s, a group of neighbours started a Reform synagogue in Hampstead Garden Suburb. Mark and I wanted to help with German refugees and stand up and be counted as Jews. So we joined this group, although I am not religious, and we rarely attended the synagogue. I tried to accept spiritual guidance from successive rabbis but realised I could not take part in any exclusive dogma. Nevertheless, we helped to start a school to teach English to refugees.

In the Reform and Liberal synagogues we now have women rabbis and every year there is a "Women's Week" and a "Children's Week". It was during one of these Women's Weeks that I was invited to preach the sermon. For me, this was the strangest and most presumptuous experience. To find myself walking from the body of the congregation up to the pulpit for my 1979 sermon was absolutely terrifying. I spoke of women's important role in Judaism and of how the tensions between men and women are "the very stuff of life, the warp and woof of positive and negative". I told legends of long ago about the complete human being, androgynous, containing all male and female attributes. I described how in ancient times, a Goddess was worshipped as the symbol of fertility and creation, the nourishing source of all life. Modern archaeological discoveries confirm the legends. In James Mellart's book *Catal Huyuk, A Neolithic town in Anatolia,* he writes: "There had been no wars for a thousand years. There was an ordered pattern of society. There were no human or animal sacrifices. Vegetarianism prevailed, domestic animals were kept for milk and wool, not for meat. There is no evidence of violent deaths. Above all, the supreme deity in all the temples was a Goddess."

Such ideal conditions could never last. In human evolution the male power must also be acknowledged. In times of war and male dominance the attributes we deem masculine are paramount. In Tunisia there are several Jewish communities who still live as in Biblical times – untouched by any contact with Polish, German or Spanish culture – and there is a synagogue on the Island of Djerba named after a miracle-working woman, The Griba. For centuries Jews came on pilgrimage to this synagogue bringing precious offerings of ornaments for the scrolls. I once visited this site. Surrounding a well in a courtyard a building of single cells provided simple shelter for the pilgrims. I could learn no more, because the Rabbi refused to talk to a woman, although he spoke French as I did!

We tend to see our personalities as definitely male or female and this polarisation is the source of much confusion and frustration. Yet, in the teachings of the Kabbalah, we find many signs and symbols of the union of opposites. The ideal human being, Adam Kadmon, combines the masculine and feminine elements which are situated on opposite sides of the body. Intelligence on the right side is male, but Wisdom on the left is female. They are described as "the two friends who never part". It is fascinating to find these ideas endorsed by modern science which shows that the left side of the brain controls the right side of the body and the more rational elements of personality usually considered masculine while the right hemisphere of the brain controls the left side of the body and the intuitive attributes usually considered feminine. We can recognise in all great men and women throughout the ages, the balance of both sides of their humanity and the acceptance of tension as a source of creative energy. Human evolution, once subject to natural forces now depends upon men and women themselves. Our masculine side has conquered and exploited and polluted the land, sea and air so that the whole planet – and even worlds beyond our own – are in grave danger, and we ourselves are the source of peril.

The most urgent need is for all mankind to balance cleverness with wisdom; to balance our insatiable curiosity, greed and selfish destructive ambition with our sense of wonder and our capacity to nurture, cherish and conserve. This balance must be achieved within each individual if it is to influence the larger world. Man has conquered nature, but still knows little of his own nature. There is a race with time if our world is not to perish.

A paramount need for our time is for liberation of both males and females from stereotypes, roles and labels. The evils of racism can be seen to have their origin in the labelling of human beings. Instead of unique individuals, we speak of Jews and goyim, Blacks, whites or yellow. We also categorise people into age or class or occupation. Instead of a single suffering, struggling person we place groups in pigeon holes labelled children, adolescents, geriatrics, mental patients, men or women.

The text for the day enjoined us to be Holy. The word derives from the same root as to heal and to be whole. How difficult it is to love and accept ourselves and others as whole persons. It is far easier to ignore the ignoble, the mean and selfish in ourselves and to project onto others, especially those we do not really know – the evil we refuse to recognise in ourselves.

Counselling is now an integral part of the healing arts – an aid in the search for wholeness. It has been said that we cannot accept in others what we refuse to acknowledge in ourselves. Compassion can only grow in us as we strive to accept all our manifold selves: the child within us struggling to be free and adult; our male qualities, thrusting, ambitious, dominant and prone to love only when demands are met; our female side, receptive, nurturing, balancing and able to cherish unconditionally, accepting our greed, hate, indifference and alienation and our generosity, love, wonder and relatedness.

We can only relate to others in love if we first relate truly with our own selves – and we are only complete by virtue of our relationships with others. Those who love us and need our love stay with us even after their death to shape our lives and make us what we are.

All living is meeting and if our meetings are not loving they are meaningless – and often dangerous. To love our neighbour as ourself is an impossibly difficult ideal, yet we can only accept the inevitable struggle and tension in this great universal truth and make it as positive and productive as we can.

In the 4th century BC, Chuang Tse wrote: "Great truths do not take hold of the hearts of the masses. And now as all the world is in error, how shall I, though I know the true path, how shall I guide? If I know that I cannot succeed and yet try to force success, this would be another source of error. Better then to desist and strive no more – But if I do not strive, who will?" His thoughts were echoed six centuries later by Rabbi Tarphon: "The day is short, the work is great, and the labourers are sluggish, and the reward is much and the Master is urgent. It may not be thine to complete the work, but neither art thou free to desist from it."

Facing Old Age and Death

The Shape of Grief
Make room for grief
And keep a hollow place
For loss; out of the common clay
Of old delight and tender ecstasy
Fashion a funeral urn
Where grief may be confined,
Looked on in calm appraisal,
There is no intruder
Thence no overflow.
Ethel Ginsberg

This is an important chapter because so few people write or think about illness and death or sensuality and sexuality in old age. A widower once said to me, "One of the hard things to bear is that nobody ever touches me now". Sometimes one has only ever been touched by one's partner. Sometimes people are not very demonstrative with children and, as they grow up, there are fewer and fewer cuddles and kisses. How often do we think of cuddling or kissing teenagers? Or grown-up sons and daughters?However much we agonise over our children's troubles and rejoice in their happiness, we do little to show it and to demonstrate physically our feelings. Almost all of us are too cold and reserved. On the other hand, some people are always flinging their arms round everybody, hugging and kissing, and many people find this offensive. How do we cope with these feelings and needs? With sensuality and sexuality which remain with many of us all our lives?

I think the hunger and the need for the everlasting arms, the comfort and support of the mother who was always available to cuddle and to "kiss it better", never leaves us. I know that when I feel ill and lonely and uncared for, I find myself still wishing my mother was with me. Our relationship was far from perfect and she died over thirty years ago, yet she was always there when we were ill, knowing what to do, knowing how to comfort and cure the ailments, especially of childhood. This longing for the loving arms – which is often mixed up with religion – surely never leaves us. I remember the poignant moments of my father's death, and of Mark's death, and of my sister's death, when my loving arms seemed important to them at that moment of parting. So touching, caressing and kissing, may not be important to everybody, but there are many old people for whom they are vital.

I often feel that with women it is the tender touch and caressing that is so much more important than anything else and maybe this is why many women turn to their own sex. So many men fail to learn how to express their feelings with the different parts of the body. There are so many erogenous zones that can be satisfied both sensually and sexually. I think men have to learn a great deal of this for themselves or be taught by their women. I found in marriage guidance that there was so little communication between people in problematic marriages that they often could not explain to each other where their bodily pleasures took place, and how to stimulate the erotic zones of their bodies. With current sex therapy, there's even more information and advice about this than there was earlier on.

Many people have been brought up to consider their bodies as evil and dirty and not made to be enjoyed but I hope this is changing as people become more liberated. Sex and love are very different things. I grew up feeling that it would be very wrong and wicked to have one without the other. Now I realise as I grow older and more experienced that sex and love are very different experiences and when you have the two together there is bliss and happiness. Yet many people have to make do with one or the other and learn to understand just what it is they are experiencing and why. In old age, one so often misses a beloved partner.

For the last two years of Mark's life we were unable to have intercourse: because of his paralysis. It was a terrible blow and occasioned enormous distress. I was so exhausted with caring for him and with maternal and protective feelings which were so much stronger than the sexual ones. I thought by the time he died that sex was finished for me and that no longer would I experience desire or be desired.

Pleasure may enhance friendship and shared memories. It is good to be companionable, perhaps to touch, kiss or to have a nice hug, although the relationship is not a sexual one. It seems to me that it is very important to be aware of one's physical needs. Many people can do without sex but few people can do without friendship and affection and this needs to be cultivated between the sexes as well as with people of the same sex.

I have not felt any urge to have sexual experiences with other women. I do like men and I do like to feel that one can still be an object of desire. It seems to me the natural thing: men and women are designed to fit into one another so beautifully, and that is such a source of ecstasy, that one should be able to continue as long as possible. Many older men need a great deal of help and stimulation, however, and quite often younger women can do this for them; but it seems to me that old couples can go on enjoying each other's bodies and finding refreshing ways to stimulate each other as they go on together.

Yet many people feel that there is something obscene or revolting about old people having sex. It is obvious that many – young people especially – simply cannot bear the thought of it! But one changes as one grows older, and one's attitudes change as well as one's appetites. Some people never lose their desire, while others give it up at different stages of their lives and don't miss it at all. I think it is very important to know both what one wants and what one's possibilities are. Unfortunately, there are so few partners for older women! They outnumber the men greatly and that is so sad.

* * *

The growing segregation of old people is a very distressing feature of our times. When you have groups of old people in homes, hostels or sheltered accommodation, they have no option but to make friends with other inmates who may have nothing in common. It is depressing to watch each other's infirmities and deaths. It seems unnatural to be segregated Surely there might be some way of forming artificial communities to replace families? One step was made in the right direction in 1992 which was designated by the United Nations as "Age Concern's Year for the Meeting of Old and Young". It seems equally unnatural for a single parent to live alone with a child, or two or three. The depression and strain that this causes, especially when there is poverty, leads to illness, both physical and mental, unless there is strong family or community support.

Some groups have come together to work like extended families but self-chosen. There is often a great affinity between grandparent and grandchild and between different generations, not necessarily of the same family. Just as I have acquired a so-called daughter in my old age, who is totally compatible, surely it must be possible to form communities for mixed age groups where each person or family has a flat or a room but where some communal facilities could be shared? Perhaps a retired person could help in the nursery groups, or in baby-minding. There should be places where old and young could come together on the basis of shared interests and not divided by age.

If one joins a class for music or exercise, art or languages, there is no age barrier. I have taken part in Local Education Authority classes where teenagers and adults and old people come together for some pursuit that they share in common and can enjoy together. The idea that because you are old you can only mix with old people is absurd.

I believe there are schemes now to 'adopt a grannie', who might be quite a useful person to have in the home. Even if she's not very mobile, she might be very helpful in, say, cooking, sewing, doing various household jobs and playing with children. She might allow the younger parents to have more free time. Anyway, it seems to me that the small, nuclear family doesn't always work very well. Indeed, the stereotype of a couple with two children and the wife at home and partner out at work is now very rare – only 5% of all households – and it might benefit from additions from different age groups. I recognise that it will not be easy to choose compatible others but I don't see why there couldn't be some training for this.

Generally, there are so many new systems of psychological self-insight and development that maybe we can work towards different forms of community living? During the war there were many examples and experiments, particularly among pacifists, and we studied these in Mass Observation. Post-war years saw the intriguing model of the Grey Panthers in the USA.

Coming to terms with age and loneliness depends primarily on one's health. To develop self-chosen interests and occupations when one is perhaps tired or in poor health is not easy but it is absolutely essential. Too often any sign of ill-health may lead to depression or panic when alone.

I was fortunate when in my fifties and suffering a good deal of pain, I discovered Dr Wilfrid Barlow and the Alexander Technique of Relaxation. After trying all available medical treatments, I found this method helped me to cope with pain and has kept me active for thirty five years. More recently I have attended classes in Tai Chi Chuan. I recommend these ways of becoming aware of the use of the body.

As a child I had often dreamed of being an artist or a musician and in the early years of my marriage I attended an art class. While pregnant it seemed especially enjoyable to work in clay. I attempted portraits and started one of my doctor, Dr Rudd. He had married my second cousin, Hannah, and we each had two sons. One day I had the clay head in the car and while I was negotiating a corner the head fell and squashed flat. I was too distressed to continue and that ended my dreams of being a portrait sculptor!

Came the war, and after, when I felt that to be an artist was pure self-indulgence, and for forty years devoted most of my leisure to politics and counselling. While Mark was ill I saw a photograph in the local paper of Dr Rudd celebrating fifty years in his practice. I thought his old, lined face more beautiful than it had been when he was a young man and was inspired to think how much I'd like to do his portrait.

Bust of Doctor Rudd

Art classes seemed a wonderful

respite from being a carer. So I joined Camden Institute. Kind friends would sit with Mark – he could never be left alone – while I attended a weekly class.

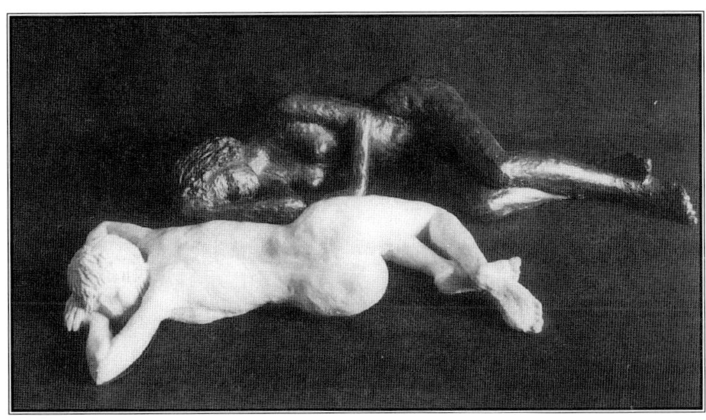

Reclining figures

Lawrence is a fine photographer and he photographed Rudd, showing the head from every angle. Eventually, Rudd was persuaded to come to the studio and sit a couple of times. The head was a great success and eventually two copies were made in bronze resin, so that each of his sons might have one.

My sculpture has remained a source of comfort in many ways, I still attend classes regularly, and my flat is full of my work in clay and stone. Carving is excellent therapy for me, more so than working in clay. I have found fossils in stones while working and to add to nature's work is a dialogue of immense dimensions. One finds meaning in the work especially if it is an abstract shape, long after it is finished.

Old age and loneliness can be transformed by new interests and creative hobbies. Even when bed-ridden one can model, paint, play chess, and write. Computers now bring new possibilities for the disabled. Music, too, not only comforts but releases feelings. My children and grandchildren make tapes for me when they discover new performances. It is so easy to feel lonely and sorry for oneself when one feels long past one's 'sell-by date' and surplus to requirements. I have experienced a strange freedom in old age and I am learning to come to terms with my limitations as well as to explore new possibilities.

Despite recent vicious cuts in funding, I find that there are still many classes I can attend in the Borough of Camden. Regular attendance gives a pattern to one's life and a focus for one's interests. It is all too easy to stay at home and to be afraid to go out alone. Joining classes not only discovers talent and interest, but one makes new friends of all ages.

Abstract sculpture in soapstone

Growing Old Disgracefully is the title of a book by a group of women who call themselves the Hen Co-op. (It was voted Best Book of the Year by *Choice* magazine in 1993). I am amused because these women are of my children's generation and, in my eyes, still young. I enjoy growing old disgracefully in my ninetieth year.

* * *

The saddest things about ageing are illness, degeneration and the death of friends. When I visit the crematorium I remember more friends of my own age who have gone than those who are still with me. The few who are still alive are frequently the source of pain as they become disabled and unable to share outings and pleasures. Deafness, blindness, arthritis, loss of memory and Alzheimer's disease all take their toll and the pleasures of companionship become sad duties. This painful stage of old age must be faced and discussed now that we live so long.

It is vital to find ways of making new friends and in old age this is difficult. If one is not able to find new people through shared interests, pensioners' groups may be the automatic answer but are not the only possibility. We must force ourselves to look into other options.

There are many clubs and societies to be explored but for me the Progressive League has been most helpful. This is an organisation that was started over sixty years ago by famous figures such as Bertrand and Dora Russell, Aldous and Julian Huxley, Professor Joad, and so on. Their idea was to unite all the groups and individuals who were striving to create a better world. They were affiliated to the Humanists and encouraged tolerance, pacifism, equality and human rights. It was felt that if all the small organisations could unite, they would have more power and influence. Over the years more and more small organisations spring up, mere drops in the ocean of progressive ideas. The Progressive League now consists mostly of older people but their frequent, regular meetings ensure an atmosphere of friendship and communion of like-minded people. Although I have been in contact with the Progressive League for very many years, it is only since Mark died that their meetings and conferences have been a source of real friendship and provided regular outings and friendly gatherings. Little did I dream, when I first attended their meetings sixty years ago that I would become their President and have been for the last few years. Currently we number about a hundred and fifty people – some married, some single – whose age ranges from young to over ninety (although most are in their sixties and seventies).

We need preparation for our later years. There are courses now for retirement but one retires not only from one's job. Women retire very often from different phases of being needed. One has most likely had a job where the role was allocated by a male boss. One has striven to fulfil the roles of lover, wife, mother, grandmother, always caring for others and playing a part rarely self-chosen. Suddenly one is faced with the fact that one is no longer needed by anybody, and a self-sufficient role has never been on the agenda.

After retirement it is not easy to find new roles which are self-chosen. It is only in recent times that women especially can expect twenty or thirty years of life after retirement. For men, too, new roles are not easy, but usually they have a woman or women to take care of them. The difference between the lot of a widower or divorcee and women in a similar position is amazing. A man living alone usually has no difficulty in finding women companions only too eager to cook for him and help with housework, laundry and so forth. Nobody seems to feel that widows need this kind of care.

It seems important to me to talk about the fears and the problems of loneliness and old age and illness. It is true that there are far too many boring old women around who are either trying to keep resolutely cheerful and repress the fears and miseries or are all too full of their aches, pains and frustrations. The more one feels sorry for oneself, the more people are alienated, yet a way must also be found to express real feelings behind the forced gaiety, which otherwise often leads to breakdown or depression. The number of people taking anti-depressants, sleeping pills and tranquillisers is quite appalling. There is a real need for groups to discuss preparation for old age and for death, which is inevitable. Lily Pincus was a great help in this respect and I miss her but we still have her books: *Death and the Family (The Importance of Mourning)* and *The Challenge of a Long Life.*

When women have retired and are looking forward to a new life of independence they often find themselves trapped because they have aged parents who now need help. Quite often all these caring roles happen simultaneously. Just at a time when a woman may herself need more rest and recreation or is about to start a new life with new interests – perhaps to take up education or develop a latent talent – parents or partners become disabled and the caring role returns. This stirs up mixed emotions which people find difficult to acknowledge. It is taken for granted that a woman is a loving daughter, yet there are many instances of abuse of aged parents just as one is now learning more about the abuse of children. One is not naturally always loving, patient, caring or willing to be on duty twenty four hours a day. It is most important to acknowledge the resentment and the bad moods and the hatred which can exist alongside the love and the compassion and the duty. It is only by facing these feelings honestly that solutions may be devised. Anyone in the position of a carer must have support. In some areas this is provided and legally help is available, but unfortunately, over recent years these support systems have been reduced.

There is an unrealistic expectation that charitable institutions may fill the gaps in the social services but during times of recession this is a forlorn hope. Nevertheless there are new charities and groups of people with similar problems get together and devise mutual help.

Where people have lived in the same area for a long time there may be a network of good friends. During Mark's long illness I had wonderful friends who would come and sit with him so that I could have an hour or two of freedom. Sometimes an old man would come and they would both have an afternoon's sleep together. Sometimes a more active person would appear to give him a meal. All the same it was hard because wherever I went, he would phone and ask when I was coming home. It was as if he had reverted to helpless infancy and only 'mother' would do. I found this almost unendurable as he contrived to make me feel guilty every time I left the house. The relationship between the cared for and the carer is never discussed openly, or at least in our case this was something Mark and I failed to do. If, at the beginning of the illness, we had been able to talk more openly maybe it would have helped. Mark often deplored the fact that he was, as he said, ruining my life, but upon looking back I see that if we had been able to be more honest he might have been less dependent.

Although as a therapist myself I knew what needed to be said or done, when overwhelmed by the situation I found it impossible to put my theories into practice and not to be controlled only by my feelings. I was fortunate in having friends who were colleagues in counselling and therapy to whom I could express my feelings but actually changing attitudes was another matter. It is so easy to be wise after the event.

Similarly, facing death is something that we should not be afraid to discuss. I had long been a member of the Voluntary Euthanasia Society, (VES), and although often Mark expressed a wish to die or to be able to kill himself, he never meant this seriously. In fact he refused to mention VES and was quite angry when I said I had joined. I have seen this conflict in many sick people. Several friends who were members of VES seemed to forget all about it when they themselves became ill and dependent. Often Alzheimer's disease prevents any clear thinking and, although the intention may have been present, it seems to have disappeared completely. Both the will and the means are lacking. Even when the mind is clear, life is very sweet no matter how painful. There is hope always of recovery, of new discoveries in treating illnesses previously thought incurable, of something pleasant happening, visits from loved ones, the opening of spring flowers, new buds on the trees, music, art, poetry. There are so many pleasures to be experienced between bouts of pain or lassitude.

I have only known a few people who have planned their death. One man, who was old and suffering a great deal of pain, decided with his wife's help to end it when the pain was intolerable and this worked with her co-operation. She herself lived to a great age and was content to be in a nursing home. Suicide is never easy and may leave relatives with unbearable guilt and grief but one can give instructions not to interfere too drastically to prolong life when it has become unendurable. The hospice movement is splendid for those who are willing to face death and the staff can be helpful in rendering this painless. For those who would speed up the process it is possible to refuse medication, blood transfusions and operations. Indeed two of my closest friends, who died quite beautifully, deliberately refused treatments except heavier doses of painkillers and sedatives. Their closest friends were with them at the end and they themselves had planned the form of their cremation ceremony and had chosen the music. They were not religious but I remember in the case of my mother that her religion convinced her that it was for God to decide and not for her to have any views on the manner of her dying.

* * *

In recent years, pleasures have outweighed the pains of old age. To make up for the years of frustration while caring for Mark, I decided to travel. To compensate for eight years without a holiday, I visited China, India, Egypt, Mexico, Prague and Budapest. I am so fortunate in having friends in France, Greece and California where frequent visits are possible, not to mention the generosity of friends in many parts of the United Kingdom.

Travelling in these far-away countries, one has to come to terms with the revelation of poverty. We take so much for granted. While enjoying exotic travel one is forced to become aware of the terrible suffering of poor people for whom the basic subsistence that we take for granted is a daily struggle. Giving money to beggars encourages crowds and does not assuage one's pain.

Despite mixed feelings about politics and poverty in far away places, I feel fortunate to have had the time, money and health in old age to satisfy my desires to see the world and its wonders. In the thrills and ecstasies of beautiful sights – landscapes, buildings and marvels of nature and of humankind – one can build up a reservoir of memories of ineffable value in old age and tranquillity.

I have seen with my own eyes and felt the magic of the history of such places as the Great Wall of China, the gorges of the YangTse Kiang, Kweilin and the River Li, the Taj Mahal by day and night, the great palaces of Rajastan, and the Himalayas. The mountains from Anapurna to Everest seemed touchable from a little plane. Taking my grandson to share the mystery and magic of Delphi and Sounion was one of my most recent precious travel experiences. In 1985 I visited Egypt, seeing the Nile and the awesome monuments to vanished beliefs and customs. I have seen astounding panoramas from the air: the Nile, a green winding ribbon in seemingly endless desert and later ice and snow and the White Waters in a bright sunlit journey over Iceland, Greenland, Baffin Island. Canada and the Rockies and the long rugged mountains and valleys of North California. We walked the miles of redwood forests, seemingly endless tracts of natural wonders. The highway that follows the coast brings one to the Getty Museum, the Hearst Castle, Big Sur and the Spanish Mission houses. Further afield, I went to visit the Grand Canyon, Yosemite, New York, Mexico and the Yucatan.

From my earlier European holidays with Mark I remember the joys of skiing before the crowds and the queues at the lifts and cable cars. I love to be alone in white wastelands, mountainous and threatening, and there is the joy of making one's own tracks in soft snow. I remember long ago climbing slowly up, herring-bone fashion, with sealskin straps fixed to one's skis, to be rewarded after the long day with a brief slalom down to base again.

Long ago and far away, memories remain of days at the seaside in England with the children, when beaches were not crowded nor roads choked with cars, always with Mark. And later, in retirement, our leisurely motoring holidays through France and Italy. To Germany, before Hitler, to Spain after the fall of Franco. To the former Yugoslavia, before the war, in the wake of Prince Edward and Mrs Simpson who first drew the tourists' attention to the then magical now so tragical coast.

How incredibly fortunate I have been. What marvellous memories and all coming together in a dazzling kaleidoscope of over sixty years in one short hour of writing these paragraphs.

There were our three fantastic holidays in Israel. Jerusalem the Golden, seen from afar as the sun set; climbing the narrow streets of the Stations of the Cross; the Dead Sea and Masada, and the ghosts of ancient Israel. In the burning heat I learnt to cool down by dipping a cotton hat in water, wherever available, in that strange land where so much history is crammed into every mountain, stone and meadow. Life on the Kibbutz and in modern cities which grow in the desert: what feelings and questions it posed to us as Jews. We could not feel that we belonged there or could imagine living there in the heat. Yet any Jew might be glad to be there given the fact that anti-Semitism does not go away and may be suffered by anyone, anywhere, no matter how much assimilated or inter-married. What is a Jew? I have written earlier about religion and the growth of the plagues of Fundamentalism, Nationalism and Racism. Sartre said, "A Jew is one whom others treat as a Jew."

* * *

Years ago socialism might have seemed to provide hope. Recent years have revolutionised all the ideologies. Human greed seems insatiable and corruption and power have made nonsense of Communist ideals which pervaded more than half the world for a time.

Capitalism and market forces provide no solution, the gap between rich and poor is widening everywhere and the politicians seem impotent. It is hard to keep hope alive in a world where growing problems and frustration and desperation lead only to violence. One fears that military or fascist dictatorships will become the favoured solutions. I often turn for inspiration to the famous dictum of Gramsci: "Pessimism of the intellect, optimism of the will." Seventy years of cruel dictatorship in the name of Communism have shown that the human spirit cannot be killed and no doubt new prophets will arise or old ones will be re-interpreted.

My own ideals have not disappeared. I feel closer to the Buddhist convictions that good and evil exist together and the evil in ourselves cannot be projected on to others: rather the battle is within. Political systems must make it possible for people to obtain the basic necessities of life before responsible communities can grow. Political institutions must tackle the inequalities and curb excessive power. Democracy, however inefficient, is the only system yet devised to accomplish this end. Therefore the Charter of the United Nations must be upheld. The growth of nationalism and wars is no solution and human rights must be defended from racism and Fundamentalism. It is all too easy to become cynical.

As I wrote this autobiography, I often wondered how I would end it. Now I know. I want to end it for myself and you, my dear unknown readers, with a quotation from a book which has profoundly inspired me. In *The Hope of Progress* Peter Medawar writes:

"We cannot point to a simple definitive solution of any one of the problems that confront us – political, economic, social or moral, i.e. having to do with the conduct of life. We are still beginners and for that reason may hope to improve. To deride the hope of progress is the ultimate fatuity, the last word in poverty of spirit and meanness of mind. The great thing about the race was to be in it, to be a contestant in the attempt to make the world a better place." He concludes, quoting from Thomas Hobbes' *Leviathan,* "'There is no such thing as perpetual tranquility while we live here, because life itself is but motion and can never be without desire, or without fear, no more than without sense. There can be no contentment but in proceeding.' I agree."